WE EXPERIENCE A CONTINUUM OF MEDIA

Published by AVA Publishing SA
rue du Bugnon 7
CH-1299 Crans-près-Céligny
Switzerland
Tel: +41 786 005 109
Email: enquiries@avabooks.ch

Distributed by Thames and Hudson (ex-North America)
181a High Holborn
London WC1V 7QX
United Kingdom
Tel: +44 20 7845 5000
Fax: +44 20 7845 5055
Email: sales@thameshudson.co.uk
www.thamesandhudson.com

Distributed by Sterling Publishing Co., Inc.
in USA
387 Park Avenue South
New York, NY 10016-8810
Tel: +1 212 532 7160
Fax: +1 212 213 2495
www.sterlingpub.com

in Canada
Sterling Publishing
c/o Canadian Manda Group
One Atlantic Avenue, Suite 105
Toronto, Ontario M6K 3E7

English Language Support Office
AVA Publishing (UK) Ltd.
Tel: +44 1903 204 455
Email: enquiries@avabooks.co.uk

Copyright © AVA Publishing SA 2003

ISBN 2-88479-016-0

10 9 8 7 6 5 4 3 2 1

Design by HSAG Design

Production and separations by
AVA Book Production Pte. Ltd., Singapore
Tel: +65 6334 8173
Fax: +65 6334 0752
Email: production@avabooks.com.sg

AVA Publishing SA
Switzerland

Sterling Publishing Co., Inc.
New York

THE PERFECT DIGITAL PORTFOLIO

STEPHEN ROMANIELLO

CONTENTS

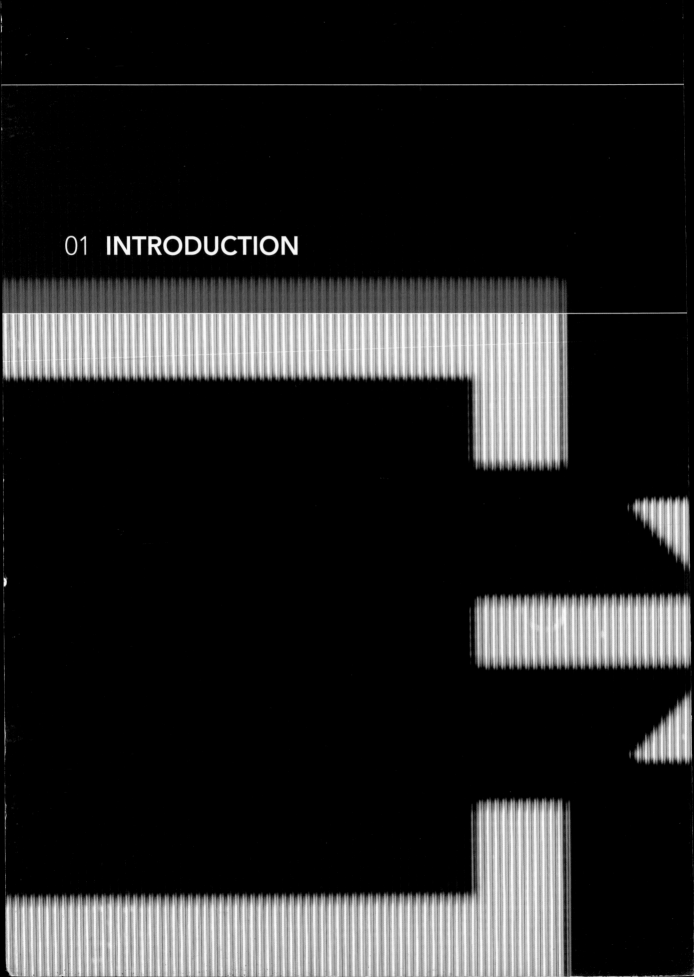

01 INTRODUCTION

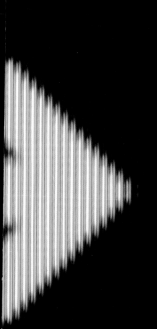

WHEN I'M DRIVING IN MY CAR AND A MAN COMES ON THE RADIO, TELLING ME MORE AND MORE ABOUT SOME USELESS INFORMATION SUPPOSED TO TRY MY IMAGINATION I CAN'T GET NO …SATISFACTION.

When the Stones sang that verse in 1965, the media's influence was beginning to permeate the fabric of western culture. Their complaint reverberated into the later part of the 20th century and indeed, what started as a trickle became a flow, and is now a flood of pictures, text and sound. In this new century, our lives have become inundated with information. For better or worse, in every facet of contemporary life – in our homes, at our workplaces and during our leisure activities, we experience a continuum of media pushed in our faces. We barely have time to take it all in no less process it. It's a phenomenon called *information overload*.

The effect of being overwhelmed by enormous quantities of useless information desensitises us to the impact of that which is worthy of our attention. We have become far more critical of the information that we allow into our realm of consciousness. What doesn't turn us on, we dismiss as noise or completely ignore. Consciously or unconsciously we scrutinise every image that we confront then, like the habitual channel surfer, nervously pressing the TV remote, we shuffle through each image until we land on one that entertains our sensibilities, stimulates our intellect or satisfies our curiosity.

THE ROLLING STONES, 1965 " "

Figure 1.0
Image taken from www.julian-hawkins.com.

The concept of information overload has changed the nature of how we present our work to the world. Those of us who depend on having our work seen, need to make a good impression quickly. We have to grab the attention of our audience and hold it long enough for them to be dazzled by our unique aesthetic vision, brilliant creativity and adroit technical skill. We need to communicate in just a few precious seconds the scope of our talent and competence. In this fast-paced, sound bite oriented culture, that's a tough order considering how many of us are out there in the world tooting our horns. This book is about choosing the fastest most efficient methods of grabbing the attention of potential clients with our message.

These days, as photographers, illustrators and designers competing for work in the dynamic, trendy and sometimes capricious media market, we must be far more concerned of how we appear. The accessibility and currency of our presentation have become key factors in communicating our talents to those who decide who gets to shoot the photograph, paint the illustration or design the annual report or website.

The Perfect Digital Portfolio was created to provide a pictorial overview of the concepts and tools used in publishing illustration, fine art, graphic design and photography to digital media and the World Wide Web. Dozens of examples of some of the most sophisticated Web-based portfolios are included in the book along with URLs and interviews with their owners. Anytime an illustration or screen shot is presented its Web address comes with it. I encourage you to check these sites out yourself for an in-depth look at how the top professionals have presented their work to the world. Also, visit The Perfect Digital Portfolio website at www.avabooks.ch/avaguides/digitalportfolio/. The book has been set out in such a way that design elements help you absorb its content quickly and easily.

ICONS

These graphic symbols are used to identify the four parts of the book. As you read you'll know exactly where you are and to what general topic the content of each page relates.

TEXT

The text explains the concepts in detail. The text is designed to be imminently readable with a minimum of computerese and jargon so that you can quickly and easily embrace the ideas and apply them to the creation of your own digital portfolio.

TIPS

Tips are ideas that will help make your work easier and more efficient.

SCREEN SHOTS

These images are taken directly from the computer screen. They might be pictures of a software interface, a page of a portfolio or a website. They provide visual examples of the concepts explained in the text.

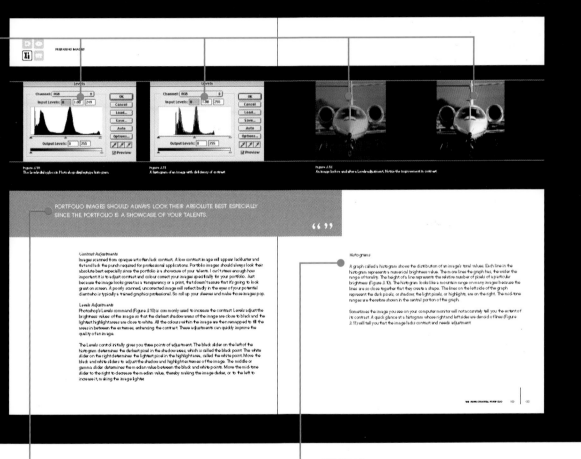

QUOTES

Often a phrase, or sentence is quoted to emphasise an important idea so that you can quickly understand the gist of a page's content.

SIDEBAR

There are many overlapping concepts that are related to the content of the book. The text in a sidebar expands upon these concepts and presents them in more detail for better clarification of the subject.

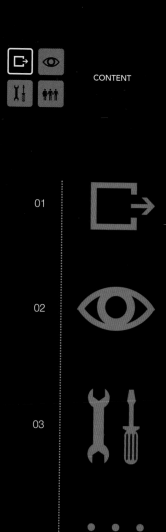

01 Introduction

The book is divided into four sections that encapsulate the many facets of the production of digital portfolios.
The introductory section explores the differences between traditional and digital presentation systems. It compares digital images to other methods of marketing, like direct mail and one-on-one interviews and discusses the advantages and disadvantages of each system in terms of the impact, efficiency, quality and content of the presentation.

02 Identity

We will delve into the essential task of presenting a cohesive visage to the world. You will learn the importance of the look and feel of a digital presentation and how it affects the viewer's response to your work. I will discuss how to determine your audience and how best to structure your portfolio for a specific client. You will learn about templates and how easy it is to modify the content of your portfolio for a specific presentation.

This section also discusses the essentials of various kinds of digital delivery systems and some of the software needed to create a specific kind of portfolio. You will be able to determine the best solution to your specific presentation goals. Should you post your images to a website, or mail a CD or other digital media to a client? Is a browser-based portfolio best for you or is your work more compatible with specific presentation software.

03 Tools

I'll explain in detail about the hardware and software you will use to optimise your images and assemble them into a dynamic cohesive presentation. You'll learn about scanning opaque art and transparencies. I'll present colour correction, retouching and sharpening techniques that maximise an image's appearance. I'll talk about image optimisation techniques that produce the best quality images and the smallest file sizes for fast downloading. You'll learn the advantages and disadvantages of the various Web formats.

This section also covers the specifics of Web-based portfolios and the software used to create them. I'll show you a number of ways to lay out your pages. I'll talk about structuring your site to take advantage of navigation and multimedia. We'll compare HTML techniques to WYSIWYG programs. I'll show you a quick method to create thumbnails from your full-size images in Adobe Photoshop. You'll see how to use meta tags to lead your audience to your site, and response forms so that a client can contact you directly. I'll also discuss the advantages of Web advertising.

You'll also embark on a tour of presentation software, and how to prepare and assemble files in presentation graphics programs like Extensis Portfolio and Microsoft PowerPoint. You'll learn about the importance of file management and we'll look at Macromedia Flash as a powerful animation machine to create dazzling multimedia presentations.

04 People

In the final part of the book, you'll be introduced to the most vital component of the digital portfolio: the people that create them and evaluate them. You'll be introduced to a group of talented photographers, illustrators and designers who use digital portfolios as a means of displaying their work to the world. In interviews you'll learn their rationales for the aesthetic and technical choices they made in producing their portfolios. You'll meet art directors who make the ultimate decisions as to whom to hire. You'll hear directly from them what turns them on and what turns them off.

Useful Graphic Arts Websites

You'll find a list of Web addresses that contain portfolios of prominent photographers, illustrators and designers. You can access their sites and see how professionals use this technology to present their work to the world.

THE DIGITAL PORTFOLIO HAS EMERGED AS THE MOST POWERFUL AND EFFICIENT MEANS OF GETTING YOUR FOOT IN THE DOOR OF A PROSPECTIVE CLIENT.

For many years the presentation of a portfolio was a person-to-person event. A photographer, illustrator or designer would participate in the ritual of setting up a face-to-face interview with a potential client. Resplendent in his or her finest professional attire, neatly preened and manicured, and sitting on the edge of the chair while the client scrutinised and judged one by one, the images contained within a bound, black portfolio.

Other traditional methods of reaching a client include direct mail of self-promotional pieces and advertising in magazines and trade publications. Both of these methods have limitations of what can be presented. Advertising space can be extremely expensive and may reach an overly broad audience, many of who may have no interest in your services whatsoever. Direct mail requires printing and postage, and once again may reach only a small number of receptive clients. Consider this statistic: the average response of most direct mail is from one to three per cent of the total distribution. Sending a thousand mailers to reach ten potential clients is not particularly efficient. Direct mail also has a limited shelf life. I wouldn't recommend abandoning these methods entirely in that they can serve as a component of *shotgun marketing*. You should consider a cohesive approach, incorporating traditional and digital methods of communication with the ultimate intention of the client ending at your portfolio website.

Digital dynamo
Within the past decade, the ability to present images has been revolutionised by the introduction of the personal computer. Today an artist or photographer can assemble, modify and transmit images, offering the advantage of instant, inexpensive distribution to a wide audience. The digital portfolio has emerged as the most powerful and efficient means of getting your foot in the door of a prospective client. In today's world you should be enlightened to the potential of using electronic media. The value and efficiency of digital portfolios cannot be underestimated to display images and communicate your presence to those who will pay for your talents.

Shotgun marketing (shŏt'gun mär'kĭt ĭ) *n.*   1. employing numerous methods to reach a client.

Figure 1.1
Background image of a digital portfolio's pages, www.robfrankie.com/portfolio.

""

Figure 1.2
A Web-based portfolio, www.bryanhelm.com.

Figure 1.3
The splash page of a digital portfolio, www.robgibb.co.uk.

Figure 1.4
A browser-based portfolio, www.marlaart.com/home.html.

It goes without saying that the quality of your work must be second to none. In every design, illustration or photograph you present you must strive for perfection. That means images should be retouched and colour corrected, sharpened and properly formatted (see Tools, Preparing Images).

Design, composition, and colour fundamentals equally apply to digital images as they do to traditional images. Great images embody the principles of design – proportion, balance, unity, direction, and emphasis. They are *balanced* in that they present an appropriate weight within a given space.

The *proportion* of the elements creates an optical rhythm that the viewer can sense. The image is *unified* by a strong cohesive force that holds it together. The eye moves fluidly in a determined *direction* and does not wander aimlessly around looking for a place to rest. Elements are structured in a visual hierarchy, which *emphasises* them in the order of their importance. The mood, colour scheme, and ambiance are consistent with the image's content. An innate sensitivity to the formal elements of the image – colour, light, shadow, form, and perspective are also imperative. Pay attention to the minutest of details with the realisation that perfection can be an illusive goal.

LOVE, PASSION, FOCUS AND SKILL ARE ESSENTIAL ELEMENTS IN THE PRODUCTION OF GREAT IMAGES.

A digital portfolio is usually a sequential system of images. There is often an initial page that orients the viewer and lists the categories of images. Frequently the images are represented by small thumbnail icons which, when clicked, produce a larger version of the image (Figure 1.3). This 'splash page' may also contain contact information and a site map.

Another method of displaying images is the self-running slide show. This can be a sequence of images that is sequenced to display for a specific period of time, called a 'delay'. There can be an intermediate transition between images that display an effect called a 'fade'.

The two most common ways of publishing and distributing digital portfolio images are to burn them on to a CD or other hard media, or to publish them directly to the Web where they will reside on a server. Each medium has certain advantages. Publishing to CD or DVD allows you to include higher resolution digital files whose quality will, in general, be better. You can also include colour-managed images that will appear consistently good on any calibrated monitor. The disadvantage of CD distribution is that the portfolio has to be mailed to the client which brings to account the obvious advantage of publishing to a website which will be accessible at any time in any place by anyone with a computer, an Internet connection and the URL.

In either case the design of the graphic user interface or GUI (pronounced 'gooy') is critical to the ease in which the images will be accessed. There are several software programs that automatically produce and display portfolio images. Extensis Portfolio, Microsoft PowerPoint and Adobe Photoshop to name a few, each offer different options for digital presentations.

Recently we see many portfolios published to hard media that are 'browser based', which means that they are published to CD-ROM as HTML files and accessed through a Web browser, usually Microsoft Internet Explorer or Netscape Communicator. The browsers offer many built-in navigational abilities including support of interactivity, multimedia animation, sound and graphics, which makes the publication of the Web portfolio much easier. It also eliminates the need to produce more than one portfolio if you choose to publish to both CD and the Web.

02 **IDENTITY**

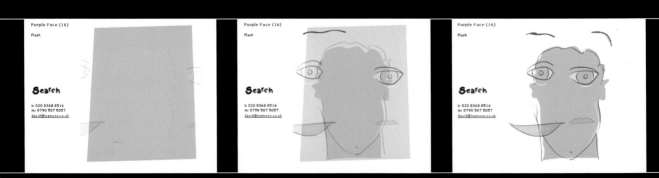

Figure 2.0
An animated sequence on www.joemoon.co.uk
by David Fathers.

YOUR PORTFOLIO REFLECTS THE SCOPE OF YOUR EFFORTS AND IS THE CRITICAL LINK TO COMMUNICATING YOUR SKILLS TO AN AUDIENCE.

You are what you do! Each day's work in the studio, on the computer, or in the darkroom refines your abilities and reinforces your talent. As you strive for perfection you become better and better at your chosen craft. In prior days it was a simple matter to interview with your black bound portfolio and show your stuff. Nowadays presenting your work requires a little more effort on your part but is much simpler for your target audience.

Some say that presentation is everything. I think that is an over-statement, however, it is a significant component of how your work is displayed to its best possible advantage. Your digital portfolio should reflect your aesthetic preferences. Every element; the layout, the choice of background colours, navigational buttons, image maps, graphic elements and type styles are important in conveying the image of you as a top professional in your field. They are all part of the gestalt of your professional identity and subconsciously influence the visitor's impression of you.

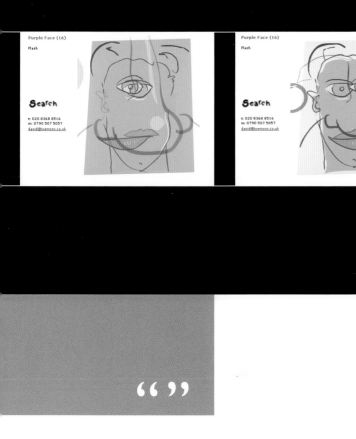

In addition to the visual image you project, the efficiency of your digital portfolio makes a difference to your client's impression of your enterprise. A website that operates smoothly with a minimum of download time, makes a far better impression than one that is slow to load and is buggy. The visitor should not have to wait more than a few seconds to access your website or CD splash page. Navigational elements should be well organised, self-explanatory and user-friendly. Images should be optimised to appear quickly.

In this section we will delve into using your digital portfolio as a means of establishing a professional identity in the mind of your clients. It covers:
• Designing for your audience
• Considering structure
• Creating an appropriate look and feel
• Choosing client-focused content for illustrators, photographers, designers and fine artists

You should present yourself as a professional entity. Projecting yourself as a business even if you are the owner, operator and only employee of a sole proprietorship communicates that you are a focused, no-nonsense professional who has the power of your organisation behind you.

Figure 2.1
Flash animated digital portfolio by www.dumdum.co.uk.

Figure 2.2
Web portfolio of Cheryl Hoffman, www.holidaychic.com.

Figure 2.3
The Web portfolio of Deborah Campbell at www.deborahcampbell.com.

What is the purpose of your digital portfolio? Ultimately, to display your images to a target audience. You are fishing for work and your portfolio is your bait. One of the first and most important questions you should ask yourself when envisioning the digital portfolio is who am I trying to reach? It will depend on who you expect your clients to be. Your work may fit into a specific niche. Take, for example the Web portfolio of Cheryl Hoffman, www.holidaychic.com (Figure 2.2). Her digital illustrations are edgy and sophisticated, and fall into the niche of trendy, chic female fashion. She is a specialist in the area of fashion (apparel and accessories), beauty (cosmetics and fragrance), spa, travel and decor. Her Web-based portfolio contains a navigation grid of colourful detail thumbnails of her illustrations, which when clicked, display full versions of the illustration.

On the other hand, Deborah Campbell at www.deborahcampbell.com creates beautiful illustrations for children's books (Figure 2.3). Her website takes a more conservative though no less lively approach which reflects the ambiance, colours, typefaces and graphic styles that are consistent with the children's book niche. Both sites are clean, professional and use the illustrations as the primary aesthetic reference.

These two websites, while displaying very different content, are designed to appeal to their target audiences. Their look and feel is client-based and reflects the aesthetic characteristics of the work contained within the portfolio.

A VIEWER SHOULD BE ABLE TO NAVIGATE THROUGH THE PORTFOLIO IN A LOGICAL PROGRESSION, AND HAVE THE ABILITY TO RETRACE HIS OR HER STEPS, OR RETURN TO THE DIRECTORY FROM ANY LOCATION WITHIN THE SITE.

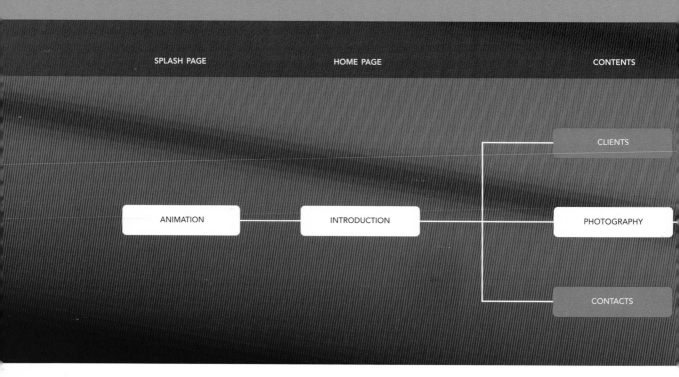

The portfolio can be structured in a hierarchy of tiers (Figure 2.4). Starting with a splash page the visitor navigates through the portfolio via graphical buttons or hypertext links. The images are divided into categories. Each category is represented by a page with thumbnails that in turn act as links to the larger image. A viewer should be able to navigate through the portfolio in a logical progression, and have the ability to retrace his or her steps, or return to the directory from any location within the site. This is a very efficient method of organising images for client accessibility and of course there are many variations of this idea.

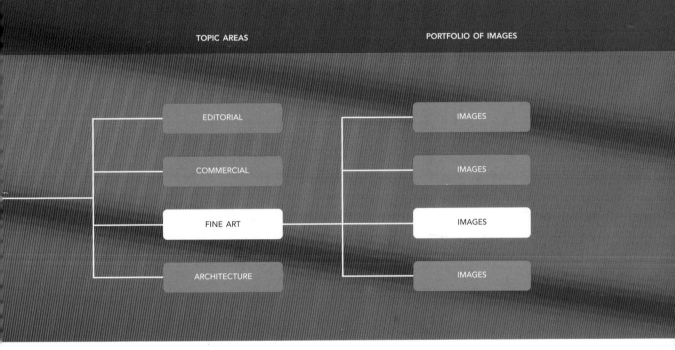

TOPIC AREAS

PORTFOLIO OF IMAGES

EDITORIAL

IMAGES

COMMERCIAL

IMAGES

FINE ART

IMAGES

ARCHITECTURE

IMAGES

Figure 2.4
Illustration showing how to structure a portfolio in a hierarchy of tiers.

Figure 2.5
Screen shots taken from www.chrismooney.com.

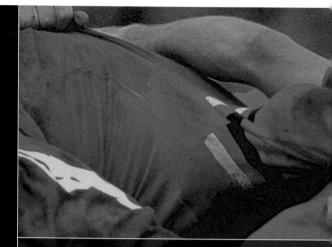

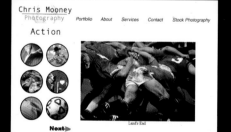

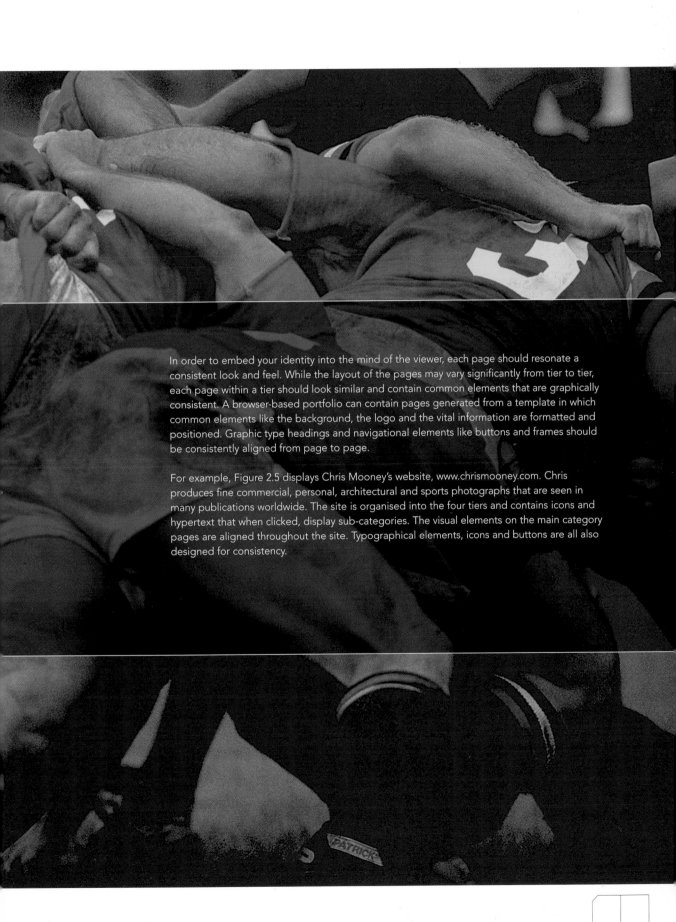

In order to embed your identity into the mind of the viewer, each page should resonate a consistent look and feel. While the layout of the pages may vary significantly from tier to tier, each page within a tier should look similar and contain common elements that are graphically consistent. A browser-based portfolio can contain pages generated from a template in which common elements like the background, the logo and the vital information are formatted and positioned. Graphic type headings and navigational elements like buttons and frames should be consistently aligned from page to page.

For example, Figure 2.5 displays Chris Mooney's website, www.chrismooney.com. Chris produces fine commercial, personal, architectural and sports photographs that are seen in many publications worldwide. The site is organised into the four tiers and contains icons and hypertext that when clicked, display sub-categories. The visual elements on the main category pages are aligned throughout the site. Typographical elements, icons and buttons are all also designed for consistency.

DETERMINE WHO WILL BE YOUR MAIN CLIENT CONTACT.

Whatever the direction of your work, it is your task to determine the images that best represent your skills relevant to a client's specific needs. Depending on the client's demands, the versatile illustrator, designer or photographer will need to gather images from a broad range and assemble them into a cohesive body of work. If your work fits into a very specific niche, you will need to organise your work into tight sub-categories. An on-line Web page or browser-based portfolio written to a CD or DVD can then be created to best display client-focused content.

Digital is dynamic! One of the advantages of a digital portfolio is that the images can be rotated or changed to display client-specific content. If you are a designer, for example pursuing a company that will be publishing an annual report, you can quickly and easily assemble a page devoted exclusively to annual reports.

Figure 2.6
An image from Julian Hawkins' website, www.julian-hawkins.com.

Initial interview
These determinations can best be assessed by carefully researching the client's intentions and goals. A critical point in this process is the initial interview, which can be conducted by phone, in person or by email. This is where you will assess the needs of the client and set the tone for future communication. It will enable you to determine which images best represent your expertise. Be prepared to take notes and to direct the conversation, but also listen carefully to what your client has to say.

Your main client contact
When you are investigating a company as an independent vendor, identify to whom you will ultimately be responsible. This person will serve as your main client contact. If freelancing for a small company, this person could be the owner or manager. If working for a large company, it might be an art or marketing director. If there is a development team, then find out which member holds the authority to approve your work, and whom you should contact if you have questions. With this information, you can assemble a body of work that reflects your expertise and experience in a focused subject area.

Figure 2.7
The portfolio website of Ramon Gil, www.ramongil.com.

Figure 2.8
Ken Laidlaw's digital portfolio, www.kenlaidlaw.com.

CHOOSE IMAGES THAT BEST REPRESENT YOUR SKILLS
RELEVANT TO A CLIENT'S SPECIFIC NEEDS.

Illustration

Illustrators usually develop an individual style. Their work is known less by its content and more by how it is rendered and its composition and colour relationships. Images may be applicable to a variety of venues yet the illustrations are usually stylistically consistent.

You can see this consistency in the portfolio of Ramon Gil, www.ramongil.com (Figure 2.7). The images are digitally rendered and have a strong division between colours and a nice retro feel to them. The subject matter varies but mostly embodies the figure rendered in dramatic lighting from a single light source with clean bold shapes.

The website is unique in that it takes advantage of the visual icon of a portfolio so as to display the images against a black background.

Notice that the portfolio is a breeze to get around, with two distinct methods of navigation including a site map boldly visible at the bottom of the page in addition to two simple arrow buttons that move the visitor forward and backward through the images. There is also a 'view larger' hypertext link that displays a screen-sized version of the image.

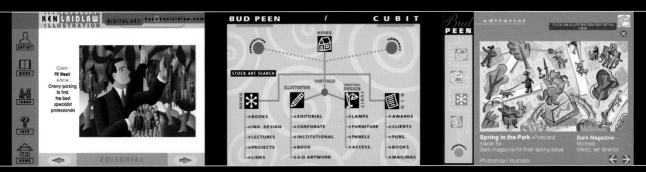

Figure 2.9
Bud Peen's digital portfolio, www.budpeen.com.

" "

Before creating a Web-based portfolio for your own work it's of great value to look at several on-line portfolios in order to generate ideas for your own. Ken Laidlaw's on-line portfolio, www.kenlaidlaw.com (Figure 2.8), makes use of several alternative ways to navigate the website. It has a series of rollover icons that change colour when a mouse is placed over them. In addition there is an on-line resume, an A to Z index, contact info and a way to get home from any page, represented by clever outline icons. In addition, navigation arrows let you move forward and backwards through the site.

Because the illustration and design career of Bud Peen is so multifaceted, his on-line portfolio presents a splash page that is a rather extensive no-nonsense site map (Figure 2.9). The site visitor is able to navigate to any category by clicking on a title. As in Ken Laidlaw's site, the navigation elements are rollovers represented by bold icons.

The sub-categories are in bold text. The main categories provide easy access to information. They include News, Illustration, Design and Biography. The Illustration sub-categories are divided into broad conceptual titles including Editorial, Corporate, Institutional, Book and 3-D Artwork. Clicking on a title reveals a template page with consistent elements that allow navigation forwards and backwards through the site.

Figure 2.10
The Tim Fuller home page, www.timfuller.com.

Figure 2.11
The portfolio's main directory, with thumbnails of various subject categories.

Figure 2.12
Content-specific pages on the Tim Fuller website.

A DIGITAL PORTFOLIO DISPLAYS WORK QUICKLY AND EFFICIENTLY AND THE BEAUTY OF IT IS IT CAN BE REORGANISED OR REVISED WITH RELATIVE EASE.

Photography

Many professional photographers take a versatile approach to their profession. On one day they may have an assignment to shoot a detail of a building for an architectural firm and the next they may be photographing promotional stills for a production of *Hamlet*. On the other hand, some photographers work within a very focused niche, choosing to specialise. Their degree of specialisation can encompass a broad range of subjects within a specific area, like architecture, or can be more exclusively focused, like commercial building interiors for example.

Your digital Portfolio

The digital portfolio serves the purpose of displaying work quickly and efficiently so that a potential client can access your skill and style and weigh the appropriateness of your aesthetic vision to the needs and goals of the specific job. One of the most obvious advantages of a digital portfolio is that its content can be quickly reorganised or revised. With pre-planning, content-specific pages can be created and seamlessly inserted into the portfolio. When designing the browser-based or on-line portfolio you should initially plan a maintenance strategy within its infrastructure so that its content is inherently flexible.

Figure 2.13
Thumbnails of images within the content specific pages.

Figure 2.14
A full sized version of an image.

Figure 2.15
An example of a mail-to link in Netscape 6.

On-line and browser-based portfolios usually open to a home page that contains a distinctive identity symbol, like a typographical logo, or graphic trademark, and contact information (Figure 2.10). This page links to the main directory (Figure 2.11). The directory will contain thumbnails of various subject categories, which will in turn link to content-specific pages (Figure 2.12).

The content-specific pages contain thumbnail images related by subject (Figure 2.13). Clicking on the thumbnail will send the visitor to the full sized version of the image (Figure 2.14). The contact information including the phone and fax numbers and the street and email addresses should be posted on all pages. If the portfolio is on-line, a 'mail-to' link will streamline the client's ability to contact you (Figure 2.15).

It is easy to be seduced by dazzling graphics and the whistles and bells of technology in the creation of a website or browser-based CD. Remember however, that the images are the focus of the portfolio and not the portfolio itself. The images should stand out prominently, ideally displayed on a neutral background. Superfluous graphic elements on the page will also create visual noise and should be avoided. Simplicity of layout and the diminished use of typography and graphics should be the goal of the page designer.

When you design your portfolio, you should plan a maintenance strategy within it so that the content is inherently flexible.

Remember, the images should be the focus of your portfolio, not the portfolio itself.

If your portfolio is on-line, a mail-to link cannot fail to make it easier for the client to contact you.

Figure 2.16
Bryan Helm's Web-based portfolio, www.bryanhelm.com, and right, an image from this site.

Figure 2.17
Jimmy Katz's website, www.jimmykatz.com.

The photographer's portfolios in the upcoming pages offer different styles of presentation. Bryan Helm's Web portfolio home page (www.bryanhelm.com) presents a stunning montage of three of the photographer's images (Figure 2.16). Enter the site and there is a cleverly designed navigation block of backward right justified type. When the mouse is rolled over the text, the images from each category appear. Bryan's work is hip and edgy and sophisticated and his portfolio contains a clean layout based on a formal asymmetrical grid that employs a clever rectilinear motif. There are several navigation elements including tiny forward and backward arrows and small rectangles which when touched with the cursor, change the picture in the image window. Bryan uses subtle, muted colours in the images he chose for his splash page. The design of the portfolio pages is also muted to emphasise the photographs.

Check out the Web-based portfolio of the well-known chronicler of the jazz scene, Jimmy Katz's www.jimmykatz.com (Figure 2.17). You'll see intimate portraits of most of the famous jazz musicians in the world. The structure and the look and feel of this site really make an impression. The site uses a bold red, black and white colour scheme to accentuate the page borders. There is a unique flashy rollover when the mouse is placed on any of the dozens of images. The site though boldly presented, lends itself to the many portraits and enhances their presentation. It is well organised with multiple navigation systems including hypertext name references to the portraits as well as image thumbnails.

While you're at the site, it's a great idea to read Jimmy's biography which presents the photographer's impetus and inspiration as an alpinist and jazz aficionado. This kind of information as presented in the Web portfolio, while personal, throws light on the artist's scope and understanding of his subjects and creates an exciting image of the man behind the camera.

Figure 2.18
Deep Creative's website portfolio, www.deep.co.uk.

THE DESIGNER'S DIGITAL PORTFOLIO CAN BE THE VEHICLE FOR PRESENTING A BROAD RANGE OF WORK IN THE BEST POSSIBLE LIGHT.

Design

The graphic designer's job description has been thoroughly transformed due to the digital revolution. At one time the designer worked exclusively for print. That is not necessarily the case today with the proliferation of multimedia and the World Wide Web. The task of the graphic designer is to present appropriate images that reflect his or her talent and versatility in a number of areas. A designer's portfolio should demonstrate a broad range of experience and the capabilities to rise to any design challenge. Designers rarely specialise in a specific area. Instead they may engage jobs ranging from brochures to annual reports to websites to books.

The designer's digital portfolio can be the vehicle for presenting a broad range of work in the best possible light. Its visual elements will impact the viewer's impression of the designer's style. For example, look at Deep Creative's portfolio at www.deep.co.uk. The black background, the use of layered transparency and the linear hi-tech identity logo convey the ultra-modern look and feel of the designers' aesthetic preferences. From page to page the text representing the categories is presented using the term 'deep'; as in deep welcome, deep down, deep thoughts and so on to provide literary continuity from page to page.

DEEP // CORPORATE DESIGN / ADS. Playstation Skatepark

Back to the corporate design portfolio

DEEP // BOOK PUBLISHING. Iz Harry on the Boat

Back to the book publishing portfolio

"

Figure 2.19
Smayvision's Web-based portfolio is a whimsical, irreverent
compilation of the design group's talents, www.smayvision.com.

BEFORE CREATING A WEB-BASED PORTFOLIO FOR YOUR OWN WORK IT'S OF
GREAT VALUE TO LOOK AT SEVERAL WEBSITES IN ORDER TO GENERATE IDEAS
OF YOUR OWN.

A very different approach to a designer's portfolio can be found at www.smayvision.com. This site is whimsical and edgy. Its splash page presents a large hotdog as the key image map navigational element.

Further into the design group Smayvision's site, there's a picture of Saddam Hussein presenting what appears to be a menu of a Middle Eastern diner. The impression this site makes on the viewer is one of an extremely light-hearted design team working in a professional venue.

The work that's displayed in the portfolio can be described as off-the-charts and irreverent, urban, madcap and hip, presenting items such as posters for the New York Underground Film Festival, a logo for MTV, CD covers for the Jimi Hendrix Experience and a variety of creative books and packaging.

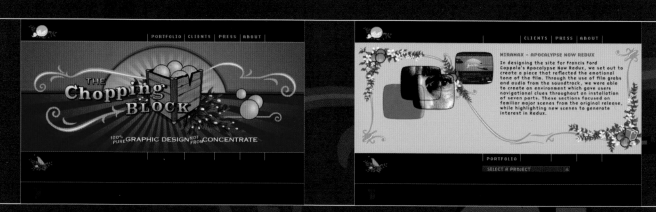

Figure 2.20
The Chopping Block's Web portfolio, www.choppingblock.com.

Another novel approach to the graphic design portfolio is the Chopping Block's website www.choppingblock.com. You'll need the Flash plug-in to see its animated and sound components. If you don't have it you can download it from www.macromedia.com. This site demonstrates the design firm's creativity and upbeat approach to its work. When you launch the site there is a graphic of a container and a peppy song about how the design firm spends its time growing oranges and working on graphic design. The song continues for quite a long time and continues to play even if you navigate to one of the many other pages. Each page contains a separate, though related, animation about oranges.

An exciting animated portfolio such as this embodies a new form of advertising and communication. It is the indirect soft-sell approach to reaching the potential client's funny bone. The portfolio presents a unique vision, quite unrelated to the concept of hiring a designer, while at the same time demonstrates in an extremely creative fashion, the information, the work and the attitude of its owners.

CLIENTS | PRESS | ABOUT

LEGO

We have teamed up with LEGO Direct on a regular basis to develop new concepts, games and online experiences for children and their parents. Utilising our original illustrations, Flash animation and programming skills, we continue to meet Lego's needs with fresh, exciting executions. All of our projects have reinforced LEGO.com's objectives of providing an online space for kids to learn and play.

PORTFOLIO

SELECT A PROJECT

PORTFOLIO | PRESS | ABOUT

FULL LIST

Adobe • AOL Time Warner • Buyarack • Commonwealth Toys • Condé Nast • The Cooper Union • EMusic • Fuelray • Guyville • Intel • Irving Plaza • i-traffic • LEGO • Macromedia • Medeski Martin & Wood • Microsoft • Miramax Films • MoMA • National Geographic Society • Nickelodeon • On2 • Phish • Reader's Digest • Restless Records • Road Runner • Roadrunner Records • Sony Pictures Classics • Tor Books • They Might Be Giants • Turner Classic Movies • TVT Records • Universal Motown Records • Viewpoint • VH1

CLIENTS

SELECT A LIST

BLOCK

100% PURE GRAPHIC DESIGN

GIANTS

OFF

Figure 2.21
Julian's abstract photographs, www.julian-hawkins.com.

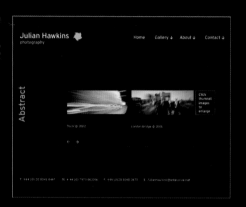

Fine Art

Many photographers, designers and illustrators may have a portfolio that has a commercial orientation with the primary purpose of drumming up business. They also may want to show off the scope of their talent by presenting an area of the site that is exclusively devoted to their fine art creations. These days, there is a thin line between fine and commercial art. Commercial art can manifest in many forms but its primary goal is to communicate a concept to an audience. It is usually fuelled by the needs of a client to advertise or entertain.

INCLUDING FINE ART IMAGES IN THE WEBSITE SERVES TO ENHANCE THE CLIENT'S INTEREST IN THE RANGE AND TALENT OF THE PHOTOGRAPHER.

Fine art on the other hand, can be considered a more personal form of work. It could include portraits, landscapes, abstractions or any myriad of subjects, but primarily executed for the purpose of self-expression. It may or may not be exhibited in galleries or museums or be for purchase, but ultimately its source is an expression of the artist's inner vision and usually represents a labour of love. If your orientation is primarily commercial but you love to draw, paint, take pictures or create digital art, it does no harm whatsoever to add a section to your portfolio that displays your fine art.

Julian Hawkins takes a very different approach to photography including both commercial and fine art in his repertoire, www.julian-hawkins.com. This is a series of abstract photographs that he has included in his portfolio. They are exciting and frenetic and done with a blithe spirit, some unconventional camera techniques and a critical eye. He features them in his website in a special abstract photography section. He also includes portraits and landscapes in two additional sections in the portfolio. These images are beautiful and compelling. Including these images in the website serves to enhance the client's interest in the range and talent of the photographer.

Figure 2.22
Marla Baggetta's digital portfolio displays commercial as well as fine art, www.marlaart.com.

Figure 2.23
The Web-based portfolio of Anna Bhushan, www.rawmango.com.

An illustrator's fine art work may fit well within the milieu of what they do in the commercial world. They may be working in an entirely different media, or they may even consider selling original illustrations as fine art. The digital portfolio is a perfect way to convey this idea to potential collectors or patrons.

Marla Baggetta's portfolio at www.marlaart.com displays an extremely refined hand when it comes to her illustrations (Figure 2.22). There is a professional consistency to her work and she has developed a distinctive illustrative style for her commercial work. Her splash page also contains links to an exclusive landscape section and we are surprised to see how versatile she really is. These images are more along the lines of work one would find in a gallery or museum with a rich, lustrous palette and a delicate brush technique. The site offers many of the original paintings for sale and also offers Giclee fine art prints too.

A more 'Fine Art' approach to a portfolio can be found at www.rawmango.com featuring the work of Anna Bhushan (Figure 2.23). The Web portfolio features beautiful poignant images rendered loosely in wet media. One feature of the portfolio is the sketchbook, which displays source images, sketches, work-in-progress and concepts. The site is easily navigable and images can be accessed by clicking on the horizontal list of thumbnails at the bottom of the portfolio.

Notably, there is no reference to commercial art in the site, and she does not refer to herself or her images as illustrations. It is not to say that these images could not be used by an astute art director or designer to illustrate a story or an editorial, however, they are presented in a form within the portfolio more as personal statements of self-expression.

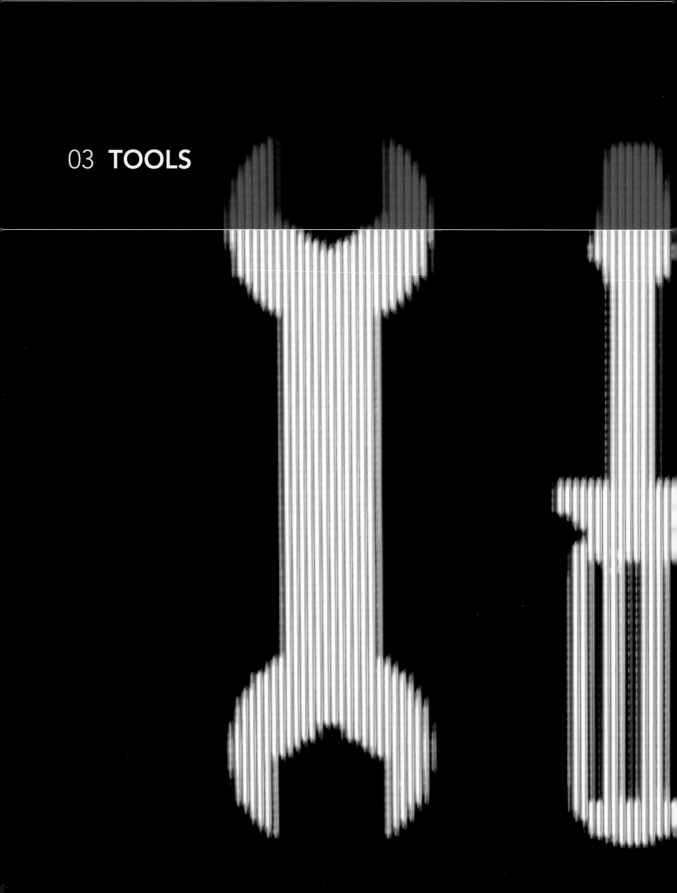

03 **TOOLS**

TOOLS

Skip Intro

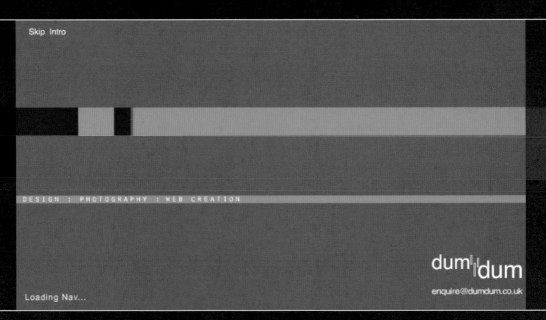

Skip Intro

DESIGN : PHOTOGRAPHY : WEB CREATION

dum dum

enquire@dumdum.co.uk

Loading Nav...

Figure 3.0
A splash screen with a skip intro option, www.dumdum.co.uk.

You've seen the potential of the digital portfolio in the many examples presented in this book. There are countless approaches to the layout and design, and what style you choose will depend on your own personal preference. The portfolio should run smoothly whether it's burned to a CD or exists on a website. The viewer should be able to access the images and contact info intuitively, efficiently and without glitches. Of course the digital portfolio should look great, enhancing and not overwhelming the work.

Many portfolios nowadays have sophisticated animations that require special plug-ins to run. If you are a Web designer, including these whistles and bells may be a key component in the demonstration to your client of your digital prowess. So frequently, a splash page that allows you to skip an introduction or turn the sound on or off will allow the viewer to move ahead more quickly (Figure 3.0).

This section of the book will present an overview of the tools, software and techniques you'll use to create a digital portfolio. It will help you consider how to best present your portfolio, whether to establish a website or burn it to hard media. We will explore the latest techniques for getting your images to look really great. We'll look at Web-based portfolios and how to create them using HTML and WYSIWYG software. We'll also investigate multimedia software to create animations, and explore well-known portfolio and presentation software.

Consider a splash page that offers a navigation scheme that gives viewers a choice.

A WEB-BASED PORTFOLIO IS ESSENTIAL, AND EVERY DESIGNER, ILLUSTRATOR OR PHOTOGRAPHER SHOULD HAVE THEIR WORK POSTED SO THAT IT CAN BE IMMEDIATELY ACCESSED BY A POTENTIAL CLIENT.

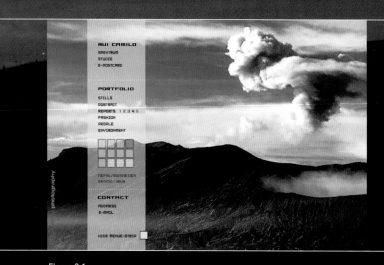

Figure 3.1
Screen shot taken from www.rui-camilo.de.

In recent years the Web has become such an overwhelming force in communication that you may ask why you would consider any other delivery system for distributing your portfolio. True, a Web-based portfolio is essential, and every designer, illustrator or photographer should have his or her work posted so that a prospective client can immediately access it. Consider a situation, however, where you need to present your portfolio under more conventional circumstances, like to a group of individuals in a room without Web access. Another scenario might be that you want to make a potential client aware of your portfolio website, in which case you could mail a sample portfolio on a disk. In these instances you might consider writing your portfolio to hard media like a CD.

As you will see later in this section, some software programs are designed to display images sequentially and automatically that have some advantages over Web portfolios. However, probably the simplest way to create a disk-based portfolio is to burn a browser-based portfolio to a CD. In other words, simply copy your HTML files and all of the supporting files and images to a disk. The client will no doubt have a browser on his or her computer, but it doesn't hurt to include the latest version of Netscape Communicator or Internet Explorer on the disk and any additional plug-ins that are required to view the images for the convenience of the viewer.

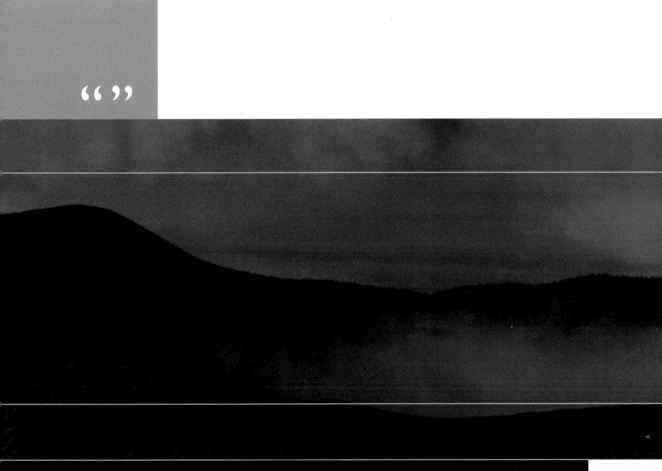

Consider a situation where you need to present your portfolio under more conventional circumstances, like to a group of individuals in a room without Web access.

Also, if you have a browser preference, you can selectively choose which one to include. Some auto Web portfolio software, like the one in Adobe Photoshop for example write the portfolio to a specified browser, and therefore, simply clicking on the icon of the home page will launch the browser. The potential client can also view the portfolio off-line by opening the home page in the browser and then using the links to navigate through the site. This is a great time saver for you in that the site only has to be developed once.

Most new computers come with a CD or DVD burner built in so writing to hard media should be no problem. Normally the process takes just a few minutes. It is critical to be sure that the files are well organised in their proper folders and structured in the same hierarchy that the HTML code has been written. See the section on Web-based portfolios to learn more about HTML.

There are two criteria that are crucial for displaying images on both Web- and media-based portfolios. First, it is imperative that your images look spectacular, and second, they must load quickly. These two characteristics can conflict with each other if certain precautions are not observed.

Scanners

The process of *digitising* the image takes place at the scanner or the digital camera. The scanner 'sees' colour and converts it into visual units called pixels. Each pixel contains numerical data. Scanning an image properly for a portfolio assures quality. Many variables can enter into the production of a quality scan. There are three general types of scanners that are capable of producing a wide range of results.

Flatbed Scanners

A desktop flatbed scanner reflects light off an opaque image. The light is analysed by a series of detectors that convert colour and tonal variations into numerical values. Flatbed scanners produce images composed of pixels. The number of pixels it can produce from the scanned image determines the quality of the scanner. For the purpose of the digital portfolio you need low-resolution images (72 pixels per inch) that keep the file size small and hence accelerate download time.

Transparency Scanners

Transparency scanners pass light through the transparent emulsions of negative film or colour slides. The quality of this light is better and less distorted because it is stronger than reflected light. The *dynamic range of a transparency scanner* determines its quality, in addition to its resolution. Transparency scanners are most suitable with a dynamic range of between 3.0–4.0 and an optical resolution of 2700–8000 dpi.

Drum Scanners

The advantage of using a drum scanner is the precision control it offers over colour balance and contrast, and its ability to scan large reflective art. Drum scanners usually produce high-resolution images and therefore they are used to create four-colour process separations. The resolution of a scanned image will usually have to be reduced to be suitable for a digital portfolio.

Digital Cameras

Digital cameras work along the same principle as scanners. They contain an array of detectors that convert light into pixels. Light that enters the camera is focused on to one of two types of detectors; the higher-quality charge-coupled devices (CCDs) and the less-expensive complementary metal-oxide semiconductor (CMOS) chips. CMOS detectors are more prone to distortion and noise.

Figure 3.2
Screen shot taken from www.rui-camilo.de.

The size and quality of the detector determines the amount of data the digital camera can collect. Inexpensive digital cameras can produce fairly good images but cannot come close to the level of quality produced by inexpensive scanners. Many photographers have included in their equipment arsenal, professional, Single Lens Reflex digital cameras like the Cannon EOS D30, or the Fuji S1 Pro which has a Nikon body that uses interchangeable lens systems. These cameras can be pricey ($2000–$6000) but offer the advantage of having high-quality images that are digitised from the get-go and therefore don't need to be scanned. The images are usually shot at high resolution. When prepared for the portfolio the resolution must be reduced.

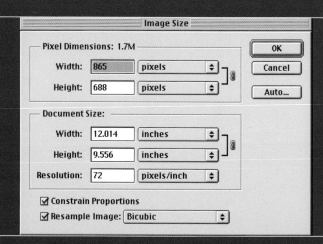

Figure 3.3
A typical scanner interface.

Figure 3.4
The resize function in Adobe Photoshop.

THE REQUIREMENTS FOR SCANNING FOR THE DIGITAL PORTFOLIO
ARE SIMPLE: HIGH QUALITY, FAST DOWNLOAD TIME.

Scanning an Image

The software that drives the scanner usually has a number of options that let you determine the characteristics of the scan. The interface shown in Figure 3.3 is for a typical desktop scanner – an Epson Perfection Photo 1650. You can see that there are many options to choose from including brightness and contrast adjustments, resolution and size controls and colour mode choices. You should scan your images in RGB mode. This will be indicated on the scanner interface probably as 'full colour' or '24 bit colour'. Ultimately the images will be optimised and the number of colours will be reduced for efficiency, but the initial scan will need to collect as much data as possible. RGB mode produces a potential palette of 16,777,216 colours which assures subtle gradations and smooth tonality. For your portfolio, greyscale and line art images should be converted to RGB also.

As previously stated, the requirements for scanning for the digital portfolio are simple: high quality, fast download time. Remember that the images are going to appear on screen so the resolution and size should be consistent with a monitor's display. That means that the image you display should be 72 pixels per inch at 100 per cent of its size.

Images for print need a higher resolution so instead of scanning the image at low resolution, scan it at high resolution (300 ppi–1200 ppi depending on its use) and reduce its resolution and image size in an image editing program like Adobe Photoshop (Figure 3.4). This will allow you to collect multi-purpose scans to be used for a variety of applications.

" "

Figure 3.5
Cyrus Deboo's website, www.cyrusdeboo.com.

Figure 3.6
Image details used as thumbnails, www.klier-art.de.

Thumbnails

While you're at it, you should resize the image into thumbnail size to be used on the site map or directory page. The thumbnails will vary in size depending on how many need to be displayed. A minimum size of one half inch of the smallest dimension is recommended to assure clarity and to display content. The thumbnails should also contain a pixel resolution of 72 ppi.

Many illustrators choose to display a detail of the image that can give the thumbnail a nice abstract quality and can serve as a visual teaser to the image's content. The effect of having several thumbnails in a grid directory can really be quite stunning as in Figure 3.6 found at www.klier-art.de.

A really efficient method of creating thumbnails is Adobe Photoshop's Contact Sheet Automation feature. From the interface, you choose an entire folder of images from which to automatically create a contact sheet. You then determine the size and distribution of the images on the page. Click the OK button and bingo! The contact sheet is configured on screen, before your eyes. You'll then have to crop the individual images to size and save and optimise them in a Web-compatible format.

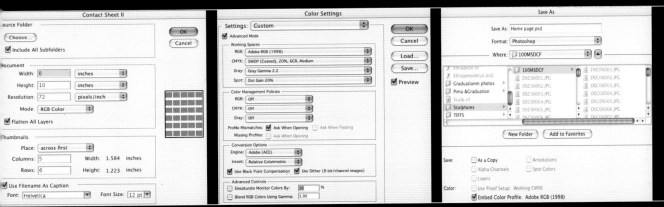

Figure 3.7
Adobe Photoshop's Contact Sheet
automation command.

Figure 3.8
Photoshop's Colour Settings dialog box displaying the
standard Web graphics SRGB IEC61966-2.1 default.

Figure 3.9
Photoshop's Save As dialog box displaying the Embed
Colour Profile option.

Colour Correction and Retouching

Rarely is an image perfect after it has been
scanned. Often, the image needs brightness
and contrast adjustments, colour correction to
remove colour casts and a bit of sharpening to
look its best. Assuming that the image was
scanned at a high resolution, it is best to make
corrections before reducing the image to
portfolio size. You can make brightness and
contrast adjustments while scanning using the
scanner's software but it is advantageous to use
a sophisticated image editing software program
like Adobe Photoshop to colour correct and
control brightness and contrast because it allows
better viewing of the image and features with
more precision control.

Colour Working Spaces

Before making corrections to an image you
should choose a suitable colour working space
and embed it in the image so that it will as
closely as possible appear similar to how it will
look on the Web or on a CD. Photoshop lets you
determine a feasible colour working space from
its Colour Settings interface found under the Edit
menu on Mac OS 9.2 and Windows and under
the Photoshop Menu in Mac OS X. Figure 3.8
displays the Colour Settings dialog box with the
RGB profile designated as SRGB IEC61966-2.1
which happens to be the default colour space
and is also the standard for images that are
going to be saved to Web or multimedia.
Assuming you are working on a calibrated
monitor, this setting will assure that your image
will appear similar to how it would look on the
average PC monitor. Assign this profile to the
image before you open the image and be sure
that when you save the image that you imbed
the profile by checking the option in the Save As
menu (Figure 3.9).

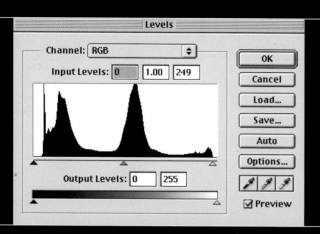

Figure 3.10
The Levels dialog box in Photoshop displaying a histogram.

Figure 3.11
A histogram of an image with deficiency of contrast.

PORTFOLIO IMAGES SHOULD ALWAYS LOOK THEIR ABSOLUTE BEST ESPECIALLY
SINCE THE PORTFOLIO IS A SHOWCASE OF YOUR TALENTS.

Contrast Adjustments

Images scanned from opaque art often lack contrast. A low contrast image will appear lacklustre and flat and lack the punch required for professional applications. Portfolio images should always look their absolute best especially since the portfolio is a showcase of your talents. I can't stress enough how important it is to adjust contrast and colour correct your images specifically for your portfolio. Just because the image looks great as a transparency or a print, that doesn't assure that it's going to look great on screen. A poorly scanned, uncorrected image will reflect badly in the eyes of your potential client who is typically a trained graphics professional. So roll up your sleeves and make those images pop.

Levels Adjustments

Photoshop's Levels command (Figure 3.10) is commonly used to increase the contrast. Levels adjust the brightness values of the image so that the darkest shadow areas of the image are close to black and the lightest highlight areas are close to white. All the colours within the image are then remapped to fill the areas in between the extremes, enhancing the contrast. These adjustments can quickly improve the quality of an image.

The Levels control initially gives you three points of adjustment. The black slider on the left of the histogram determines the darkest pixel in the shadow areas, which is called the black point. The white slider on the right determines the lightest pixel in the highlight area, called the white point. Move the black and white sliders to adjust the shadow and highlight extremes of the image. The middle or gamma slider determines the median value between the black and white points. Move the mid-tone slider to the right to decrease the median value, thereby making the image darker, or to the left to increase it, making the image lighter.

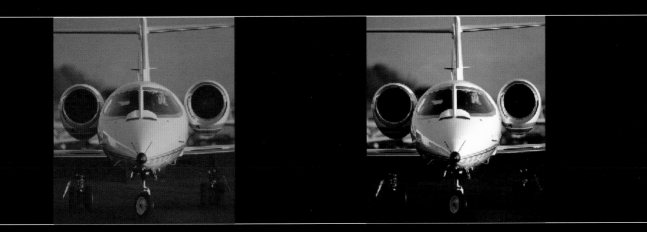

Figure 3.12
An image before and after a Levels adjustment. Notice the improvement in contrast.

Histograms

A graph called a histogram shows the distribution of an image's tonal values. Each line in the histogram represents a numerical brightness value. The more lines the graph has, the wider the range of tonality. The height of a line represents the relative number of pixels of a particular brightness (Figure 3.10). The histogram looks like a mountain range on many images because the lines are so close together that they create a shape. The lines on the left side of the graph represent the dark pixels, or shadow; the light pixels, or highlights, are on the right. The mid-tone ranges are therefore shown in the central portion of the graph.

Sometimes the image you see on your computer monitor will not accurately tell you the extent of its contrast. A quick glance at a histogram whose right and left sides are devoid of lines (Figure 3.11) will tell you that the image lacks contrast and needs adjustment.

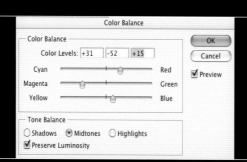

Figure 3.13
The Colour Balance dialog box.

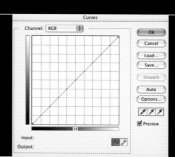

Figure 3.14
The default Curves dialog box.

Removing Colour Casts
Frequently, an image will attain an overall colour cast either from poor lighting or from properties of the scanner. Photoshop's Colour Balance command is used to adjust the overall mixture of colours in the image and especially to eliminate colour casts.

The dialog box (Figure 3.13) presents three colour sliders. Each colour slider represents two colour opposites. By increasing the amount of a specific colour (by moving the slider towards its name), you, in effect, decrease its opposite. Therefore, if you add red to an image, you effectively decrease cyan. If you add blue to an image you decrease yellow and if you add magenta you decrease green.

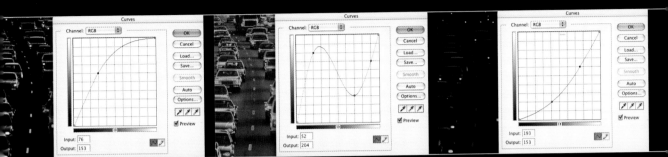

ree different Curve adjustments can produce a wide range of effects.

Adjusting Brightness Curves

For precision colour, adjusting an image's brightness Curves offer Photoshop's most powerful adjustment tool. With Curves, you can adjust an image's brightness Curve to lighten or darken an image, improve its contrast, or even create wild solarisation effects. Where as Levels gives you a limited range of brightness to modify, Curves allows you to adjust any range of brightness.

When you open Image > Adjustments Curves, Photoshop displays the Curves dialog box (Figure 3.14).

The Grid

If you click on the centre of the diagonal line in the Curves dialog box and drag it toward the upper-left, you will lighten the image. If you bend the line toward the lower right, you will darken it. If you perform either of these operations, you are altering the position of the mid-tones. A classic S curve will increase the contrast of the image by darkening the shadows and lightening the highlights.

Figure 3.16
The effects, from top to bottom, of dodge, burn, desaturate and saturate.

Figure 3.17
Photoshop's Unsharp Mask filter dialog box.

Figure 3.18
The before and after image sharpened with the Unsharp Mask filter.

Dodging, Burning, Saturating
Image editing tools that affect the colour of a picture are derived from traditional darkroom techniques. Use these tools to manually darken, lighten or intensify or subdue areas of colour. They are essential because you can focus the technique on a specific area depending on the brush size and exposure or pressure you choose. In Photoshop you set the exposure or pressure in the Options bar. It is recommended that you apply these tools in multiple passes with small exposures or pressures to gain control and produce results gradually.

The Dodge Tool
Lightens areas. By passing the tool over an area several times, areas can be made to stand out against their darker surroundings.

The Burn Tool
Darkens areas. Pass the tool over an area to darken the shadow areas and push back the detail.

The Sponge Tool
Saturates or desaturates areas of colour. Pass it over an area and watch the colour intensify or become a totally desaturated grey.

Sharpening your Images

In Photoshop, or any other image editing software like Corel Image Studio or Macromedia Fireworks, the final step in preparing your portfolio images before saving them to a Web-compatible format is to sharpen them using the Unsharp Mask (USM) filter. This filter is actually a contrast-adjustment tool that works as part of the colour correction workflow and if used properly, it can really make your pictures 'pop' (Figure 3.18).

USM increases the transition in areas of highest contrast and leaves the areas of similar contrast unaffected. By increasing the contrast of an image it fools the eye into thinking soft areas are in focus.

In Photoshop, apply the USM, by choosing Sharpen > Unsharp Mask from the filter menu. The dialog box (Figure 3.17) displays a thumbnail of the image.
To apply the USM, move one of its three sliders:

1. Amount
   Determines how much sharpening will be applied. In order to see the effect, however, you must also apply a Radius.

2. Radius
   Controls the width of the sharpened edge. Lesser values produce thinner edges while greater values produce wider edges with more overall sharpening.

3. Threshold
   The slider restores softer portions of the image. Too much Threshold may reverse the effect of the USM.

Unsharp to Sharpen?

Optical techniques were once performed in a process camera in ancient times before computers. A piece of film was cut to mask areas of images when they were being 'bumped' or exposed to increase their contrast. Flesh tones and other soft areas were unaffected while the contrast of the boldest edges would be pulled into sharp focus. The area within the mask was protected. The area outside the mask was being sharpened hence the term *unsharp* mask came into being.

Apply the minimum amount of the USM filter to achieve the best possible results without over-sharpening which can blow out areas, shift colours, and create dark or light halos and increase noise and artefacts.

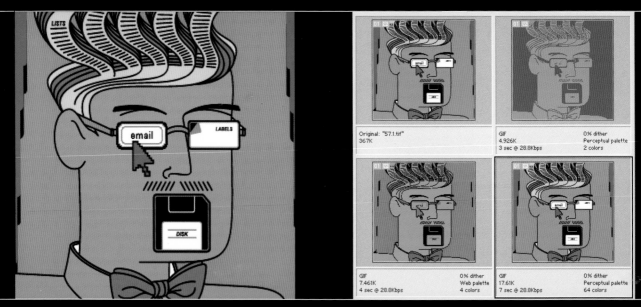

Figure 3.19
A vector illustration from www.cyrusdeboo.com.

Figure 3.20
An illustration comparing several different GIF colour settings. Notice the difference in quality efficiency and download time compared to the original.

Formatting Images

Once your images have been scanned, sized, colour corrected and sharpened, they are ready to be optimised for performance within the digital portfolio. How you optimise them will best be determined by their content and application. For browser-based portfolios, you'll optimise your images in GIF, JPEG or PNG format. GIF and JPEG are compatible with most browsers but PNG, while offering many advantages, is compatible only with recent versions of Netscape and Explorer.

GIFs

GIF stands for Graphic Image Format. GIF format is best applied to images that have large areas of colour like vector illustrations similar to the one in Figure 3.19. GIF reduces file sizes of an image by adjusting its *bit depth* or the number of colours that the image is capable of supporting. Compare the images in Figure 3.20 with different colour settings. The one in the upper left corner is the original unoptimised image. Note its file size. To the right is an optimised GIF with a bit depth of eight. In the lower left is the same image with a bit depth of 32 and in the lower right, the image has a bit depth of 128.

JPEGs

JPEG stands for Joint Photographer's Experts Group named after the team of photographers that developed the format. For photographs and any image with significant amounts of gradations in light or shadow, JPEG is the file format of choice for the best look and compression. You can optimise an image as a JPEG to produce the best results for your photographs yet JPEG format can have its drawbacks. JPEG format is a lossy compression mode; it reduces file size by discarding image data which can severely affect the quality of an image. Figure 3.21 shows the extremes of JPEG compression. You'll want to compare the image before settling on a setting. Making these kinds of decisions is the heart-and-soul of image optimisation for the Web. It's always a balance of good looks and quick load times, and always based within the context of the page with which you are working.

JPEG	60 quality	JPEG	0 quality
102.3K		17.54K	
37 sec @ 28.8Kbps		7 sec @ 28.8Kbps	

Figure 3.21
The extremes of JPEG settings. Notice the deterioration and artefacts in the image on the right, set to JPEG Low at the expense of image quality. The image on the left maintains quality set to JPEG High.

Usually the process of optimisation means elimination of colours or image data and image compression which results in smaller file sizes and hence, faster download times. Many image editing software programs offer options that will allow you to compare the quality and efficiency of images in a variety of formats and settings like Adobe Photoshop's Save Web Option.

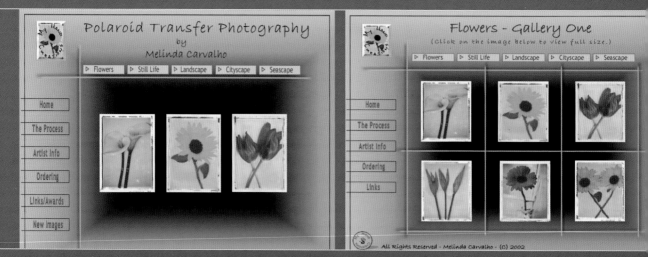

Figure 3.22
Website of Melinda Carvalho, www.myhandcreations.com.

You are a photographer, illustrator, or graphic designer who has spent countless hours mastering your craft, and even if your medium is conte crayon or Polaroid film (see Polaroid artist Melinda Carvalho, www.myhandcreations.com, Figure 3.22), you've decided to go digital to find an audience for your work. The computer revolution has not only spawned an entirely new marketplace for visual imagery, but is the basis of an incredible distribution network which can help you find new audiences for your artwork unmatched by the scope of conventional galleries and advertising. You have honed each of your images to perfection, and while you may or may not have used computer software such as Photoshop, Freehand, Illustrator or Flash to create a body of work, now is the time to turn to the computer in order to assemble a presentation. Let's take a look at some software which can help put your plans into effect.

Still Life - Gallery One
(Click on the image below to view full size.)

▷ Flowers ▷ Still Life ▷ Landscape ▷ Cityscape ▷ Seascape

Gallery One
Gallery Two

Home
The Process
Artist Info
Ordering
Links

Cityscape - Gallery One
(Click on the image below to view full size.)

▷ Flowers ▷ Still Life ▷ Landscape ▷ Cityscape ▷ Seascape

Home
The Process
Artist Info
Ordering
Links

USING THE FILE BROWSER ALLOWS YOU TO QUICKLY SELECT THE IMAGES YOU WISH TO PLACE IN A FOLDER TO PRESENT TO A POTENTIAL CLIENT, AND BATCH RENAME OR ROTATE THEM AS YOU GO.

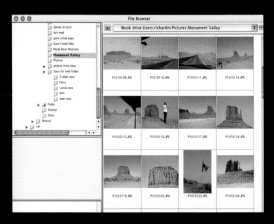

Figure 3.23
The Photoshop File Browser Expanded view.

Figure 3.24
The Photoshop File Browser Unexpanded view.

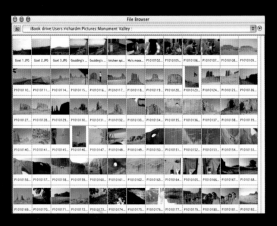

Adobe Photoshop

As we've seen Adobe Photoshop is best known for its extensive image editing capabilities, but it also contains several features to assist you in managing and presenting a collection of images. Let's take a look at the File Browser and Automate functions, and how to apply them to portfolio building, management and presentation.

The File Browser is Photoshop 7's powerful new image viewing feature, allowing you to view folders and graphic files in a variety of formats. Images can be sorted, renamed, rotated, moved to new folders and deleted, all without ever leaving the browser window. To open the File Browser, choose File > Browser (Mac) or Window > File Browser (Windows), or, by default, the File Browser is displayed in the palette well when working in screen resolutions of 1024 x 768 or higher. In Photoshop's characteristic style, many of the commands are accessible in a number of ways, so that you can tailor use of the browser to your individual approach.

Once opened, default mode presents a palette with the file folder hierarchy shown in the upper left portion of the window, with windows for the currently selected file or folder and file information below, and the gallery windows to the right show the contents of the currently selected folder (Figure 3.23). By clicking the small triangle in the upper right corner of the palette or on the file browser tab, you can open the main commands menu. Here, you will find the basic commands which determine your working environment. By unchecking Expanded View, the palette layout as described above changes to a single window (Figure 3.24), which shows only the gallery of images and folders. By deselecting Show Folders in the menu, only the graphic files in the selected folder will be displayed. This option gives you the advantage of scanning through the greatest number of images quickly.

As always with Photoshop, you are seldom more than a keystroke or two away from the features of either view. Here's how: At the bottom of the File Browser palette is another group of pop-up menus and toggle switches. They allow you to again, switch between Expanded and Gallery views, to change the proportions between views, to toggle between information windows, to

choose a variety of sort options, to change view options and to rotate images. When selecting items to place in a folder you can select all the images in a folder, select a sequential number of images by clicking on the first image and shift-clicking on the last image, or select non-sequential images by selecting the first image and Command (Alt) clicking on subsequent ones and dragging them to their new folder. Using these features, you can quickly select the images you wish to place in a folder to present to a potential client, and batch rename or rotate them as you go.

The bottom line is this – using any combination of techniques you wish, the File Browser allows you to view your images at a glance, sort them through a variety of methods, and place them in appropriate folders, making them ready for the next step, presentation.

Avoid downloading more than one series of images of the same type into the same folder without renaming the frames (P1010001.JPG…P1010045.JPG, for instance), as the second file may overwrite the first, requiring luck and software to retrieve the first set of images.

POWERPOINT IS A LARGE GENERIC PROGRAM, WHICH WHEN USED WITH SOME DISCRIMINATION CAN BE A VERY POWERFUL PRESENTATION TOOL.

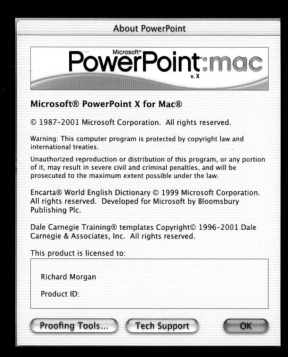

Figure 3.25
The PowerPoint splash screen.

Figure 3.26
The PowerPoint interface.

PowerPoint

Microsoft's PowerPoint (Figure 3.25) is the most widely used presentation software in the business environment, and as such it may provide you with the best vehicle for interesting a team of potential clients in your work. Its familiar slide show format allows you the opportunity to prepare a 'guided tour' of what services you can provide. Due to its widespread use in conjunction with video projection systems, PowerPoint may provide you with the best means of introducing your work to a group, with the added advantage that they may well be viewing it at a larger scale than a computer screen. If you are not invited to make the presentation yourself, your graphic presentation can easily be transferred to CD (or to the Web), where, hopefully, one of your advocates will take advantage of PowerPoint's familiar yet proven features.

Upon opening PowerPoint, you will be presented with a variety of slide show templates, many of which might not be of appropriate use to you (Figure 3.26). PowerPoint is a large generic program, which when used with some discrimination can be a very powerful presentation tool. That being said, let's cut to the quick and concentrate on getting a slide show of your featured work on screen. Assuming that showcasing your own graphic or photographic work is your primary goal, let's step through a sample process. When you launch the program, you see the Project Gallery interface. This time, you will be asked to select from a number of slide layouts, with a variety of text, animation and picture formats.

You may create slides by double-clicking on the image window and navigating to the image, or dragging and dropping from your favourite image display program. The default screen leaves a white border around the image, but you can change the background colour or use the control handles to scale the image to the window. To continue, select Insert > New Slide. Once you have assembled your slides, under the Slide Show menu, you can select from a lengthy list of Transitions, but, unfortunately, only in three speeds. My advice would be to keep it very simple, unless you are very familiar with your client's tastes or sense of humour. To view your show, just select Slide Show > View Show and start tweaking!

Choose 'Large Picture'. In this way you will be creating a full-screen slide show that lets the images speak for themselves.

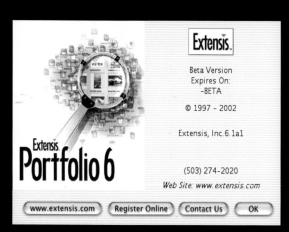

Figure 3.27
Extensis Portfolio splash screen.

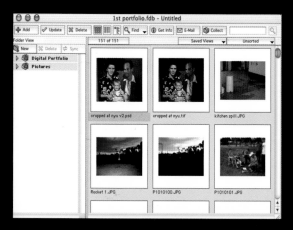

Figure 3.28
Portfolio's cataloguing feature.

Extensis Portfolio

While both Adobe Photoshop and Microsoft PowerPoint offer a number of useful filing options, Extensis Portfolio (Figure 3.27) is a dedicated graphic file management system, with extensive cataloguing capabilities. Its File Sync features and floating master palette give the user the greatest flexibility if assembling a targeted portfolio from a number of files or you have a frequent need to access collections of archived materials quickly. Just dragging and dropping any volume's contents on to the portfolio window will catalogue the item catalogued (Figure 3.28), whether it is a folder from your hard drive, a CD, or a ZIP or JAZ disk. And, your newly created catalogue puts all this information at your fingertips, whether the removable media is present or not.

The thumbnails of all the images are catalogued in addition to any embedded information from the digital camera, scanner source or editing software. An easy-to-use menu gives you a variety of additional cataloguing options, including the best keyword assignment capabilities of any of the software I have used. A picture may be worth a thousand words, but a few keywords accompanying large numbers of images can make sorting and retrieving just the right picture much less daunting.

In addition, you are provided with a box for descriptive text, the ability to copy, move and rename single or grouped images, and a variety of sort options. Administrators have access to a Fields category, where other identification and filing options are customisable. But even more impressive is Portfolio's File Sync feature, which, with the press of a button, updates all of your file content information. In this way, you can reorganise files, dragging and dropping images into new or different folders, and File Sync provides an updated catalogue of the changes you have made. Despite all the reorganising you have done, you may still have trouble finding that perfect image you know you have in the maze. That's why Extensis Portfolio also provides an excellent Find feature to support its cataloguing arsenal, offering a customisable window to refine your searches.

Now that you have all that information in front of you and you have chosen your best work, you may still notice a flaw, or decide that an image should be cropped for its application in the current collection you are assembling. No problem! Just press Command E (Mac) or Control E (Windows), and Portfolio launches your editing program and opens the desired file, or you can even edit in a different program than the source file by dragging the image on to the icon of your alternate software.

While Portfolio's strongest selling points are its access and organising capabilities, it also includes excellent slide-show and publish-to-Web features, making it a very desirable distribution program as well.

Figure 3.29
A portfolio site with text links, www.fluxstudio.com.

Figure 3.30
A portfolio site with bold information 'chunks', www.frostdesign.co.uk.

PLANNING AT THE INITIAL STAGES WILL PAY OFF
IMMEASURABLY IN THE LONG RUN.

The Web portfolio is perhaps the best means of communicating your talents to a prospective client for a number of reasons. It offers instant access to your materials. It can be updated at a minimum of time and expense, and it can provide a vehicle for your clients to express an interest in your work and directly communicate to you their desire to do business.

The Web is such a dynamic publishing medium and so commonplace that it is essential for every designer, illustrator and photographer to publish their work on-line. Art directors, agencies and professionals in the advertising field expect to be able to easily access your site and view your work.

Planning
Putting together a website can be a formidable task, but planning at the initial stage will pay off immeasurably in the long run. Start by listing goals of the site. Write these ideas down on paper to focus your intentions. Many sites are assembled by a group of talented specialists including a copywriter, a graphic designer, a multimedia specialist and a programmer. It is of great value to brainstorm with the design team or other members of your business. A brainstorming session should include some strong coffee and a flip chart and a marker pen. Ideas are written down on the flip chart, no idea being too absurd for consideration. Ultimately the ideas will be synthesised and distilled into a cohesive concept.

Once a concept is devised, a blueprint is drawn up in the form of a flow chart that reflects the navigation strategy. Rough layouts of the page templates are sketched, and logos and other graphic elements are designed and saved. Copy is written and all portfolio images are optimised and saved in the appropriate size and formats. Once all of these elements are prepared, the process of assembling the website can begin.

Figure 3.31
A portfolio with a strong grid structure, www.giacomettidesign.com.

Figure 3.32
An attractive image-heavy site, www.segura-inc.com.

Layout

The visual organisation of page elements is crucial to the appearance and performance of the site and to its overall look and feel. You must decide how you would like the site to fill the monitor screen. Will the information utilise multiple text or graphics links navigated by clicking on a button or on text as in the website at www.fluxstudio.com (Figure 3.29) or will the pages be simpler and contain information chunks as in www.frostdesign.co.uk (Figure 3.30)? Other layout methods may include a sophisticated grid structure with seemingly independent, interactive units as in www.giacomettidesign.com (Figure 3.31) or attractive image-heavy websites like www.segura-inc.com (Figure 3.32). Whatever layout options you choose, the site should follow the basic tenets of graphic design. The viewer's eye should move with fluid ease over the contents and rest on areas of emphasis. The proportional relationships of elements should create an optical rhythm throughout the layout. The composition should be held together by a

strong cohesive force and unified by mood and colour. The site should appear clean and uncluttered. Avoid cramming too much on to any one page; instead deliver the information in palatable 'chunks'. Build the essentials into the page and avoid miscellaneous frou-frou.

Normally, a Web page is built to a width of 768 pixels, designed to fill the horizontal dimension of a 17" monitor. Some designers will lay out the live material 585 pixels wide to accommodate the horizontal size of a 13" monitor, but this practice is less common nowadays. The depth is going to depend on how you deliver the information. If you've chosen a scroll type layout then the site visitor can scroll down the page a reasonable number of times to access the information. A better portfolio will display the information in cohesive, content-related visual units, in which case, the page should not exceed 360 pixels in depth.

Figure 3.33
The Web portfolio of Ramon Gil displaying how a template can be used, www.ramongil.com.

Templates

Another layout option can communicate the impression that specific page elements are dynamic while others are static. For example, in www.ramongil.com (Figure 3.33) the images within the portfolio seem to change while the common elements like the logo, the text, the navigation buttons and the outer border are all in position.

Each page on a website is a separate document. The method for producing the illusion of changing page elements employs page templates. An initial page layout is designed and all of the common elements are positioned within the document. These can include borders, logos, backgrounds and other graphic elements. This document is copied and used as a template for each page. The images are aligned for consistency. Usually there is a button that transports the viewer to the next image. When the button is clicked, the entire page changes but only the dynamic elements appear to change.

Figure 3.34
The source code of a Web page, www.lallophotography.com.

Figure 3.35
The Web page as it appears on the browser, www.lallophotography.com.

HTML

Hyper Text Markup Language (HTML) is the code that browsers like Netscape Communicator or Internet Explorer can read. Most Web pages have a core HTML structure underlying what you see on screen. HTML code can be written on the simplest text editor software like SimpleText for Mac or Notepad for Windows and saved as a document with an HTML extension. HTML can also be written in word processors like MS Word or WordPerfect.

Some old timers – professionals who've been building Web pages for more than five years – still write in HTML claiming that the code is less heavy, cleaner and hence, faster to download with fewer problems. With sophisticated WYSIWYG (What You See Is What You Get) programs you don't have to be an HTML programmer to assemble a Web page. It is helpful however to know a few things about the markup language in order to get an idea of how it works.

HTML code consists of *tags* – commands that tell the browser how to treat text or graphics files. HTML tags are enclosed in brackets that are entered with the greater than and lesser than symbols on a keyboard, for example, <HTML>. There are two types of tags, a beginning tag; <HTML> and an end tag; </HTML>. The object affected by the tag, like text for example, is contained between the beginning and end tags. The tags are clustered so that multiple tags bracket each other. For example, if you want to designate bold, italic text that is centred on the browser page, the HTML code will appear like this:
<CENTER><B><I>My Web Portfolio</I></B></CENTER>

It makes no difference what case, font, or type weight you use to write HTML tags, however, the content you enter between the tags is case sensitive. Some programmers choose all caps for the tags because they are more easily identifiable in long columns of text. How you apply line breaks to the code is also irrelevant. To apply a line break to the document so that the browser can read it requires a line break tag or the use of *tables*. You can enclose multiple commands. For example, the body tag can contain information about a background, a font, and a font colour:
<body background="tilepattern.gif", font="Helvetica", color="ff6600">My Portfolio Page

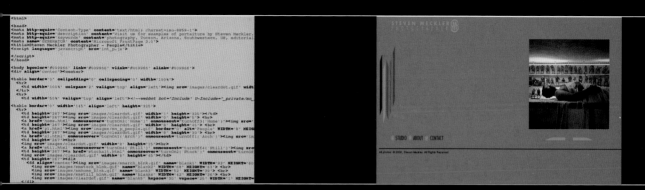

Figure 3.36
When there are rollovers, multiple images, a table structure or multimedia, the HTML code can be quite complex. As you can see this page was programmed in Microsoft FrontPage.

Figure 3.37
The People page of www.mecklerphotography.com as it appears on the browser.

In this instance the following information is being communicated to the browser: the background is using a tiled GIF image named tilepattern.gif, the font is Helvetica and the colour is the hexadecimal colour ff6600. Each command is followed by an equal sign, and the specifying information, called an *argument* is in quotes. 'My Portfolio Page' is the text that is being affected; notice that it is outside the tag. Images can be entered into the code in a similar fashion using the tag: <img src="roses.jpg">. This tag refers to the image named roses.jpg stored in a folder with the HTML document at the same level in the hierarchy.

Usually, HTML is constructed within a basic 'shell' that contains the structure of the page. The shell looks like this:

```
<HTML>
<HEAD>
<TITLE>
</TITLE>
</HEAD>
<BODY>
</BODY>
</HTML>
```

The head tag contains the information that identifies the site. Key words called *meta tags* that identify the site to a search engine may be entered into the head section of the code. If the site is registered with the search engine, the key words can lead the potential viewer to the site.

The body of the code is where its content is determined. All the tags that designate the specifications for background colours or images, pictures, text, buttons, links and multimedia are entered here. Figure 3.34 displays the source code for a simple portfolio Web page found at www.lallophotography.com. Notice the shell structure and placement of tags.

Browsers can be unforgiving about HTML code. It is essential that the code be accurately entered, especially when placing images. The name of the image must be spelled exactly and is case sensitive. The equal sign and quotation marks must be in place with no additional spaces.

Figure 3.38
Table tags in an HTML document.

Figure 3.39
Java Script in an HTML document.

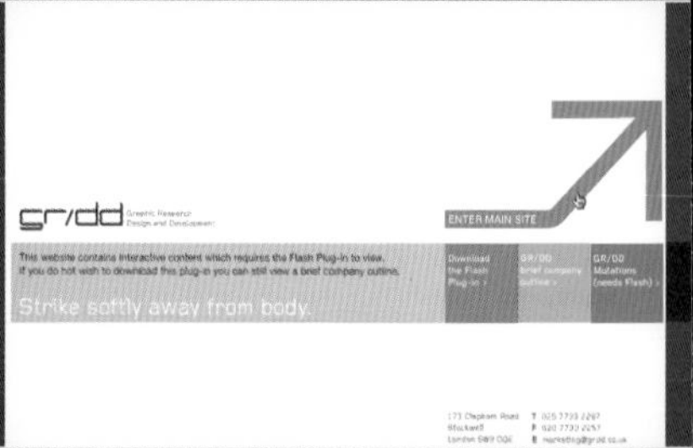

Figure 3.40
The effect of a Java Script rollover on a Web page, www.grdd.co.uk.

Graphic Research

HTML Tables

Tables are the primary armatures for Web pages. They are the skeleton to which all page elements are attached. Tables are responsible for the horizontal and vertical layout of elements and their position on the page. Tables create a rectilinear container for the placement of yet smaller rectilinear cells. Each cell contains the content of the Web page. By careful placement of content within tables without borders, a page with a sophisticated asymmetrical layout can be achieved.

The table structure always begins with <TABLE> and ends with </TABLE>. You'll also see values for the width of the table (its total horizontal dimension in pixels and its *border*). You'll also see specifications for *cellpadding* which sets the amount of space, in pixels, between the sides of a table cell and its contents, and for *cellspacing*, which sets the amount of space, in pixels, between the exterior frame of the table cells.

When you observe the source code of almost any Web page, you'll also see the ubiquitous table tags – TD and TR (Figure 3.38). The <TR></TR> tags stand for Table Row which begins or ends a horizontal row of cells. The <TD></TD> indicates the Table Data tag which determines the placement of content within a cell.

Java Script

If you look at the source code you'll see Java Script whenever there is multimedia or certain types of interactivity on a Web page (Figure 3.39). Rollovers for example, are produced by Java Script code. A rollover is an action that is initiated by the hovering or clicking of a mouse. The Java Script can be quite lengthy and for a very good reason – it contains complex commands to load and unload images quickly to produce the visual change on a specified area of the image. Fortunately you don't have to be a programmer to enjoy the benefits of Java Script. All of the WYSIWYG programs offer the ability to create and edit rollovers and other multimedia operations.

WYSIWYG PROGRAMS RESEMBLE DESKTOP PUBLISHING PROGRAMS, THE DIFFERENCE BEING THAT WHILE YOU LAY OUT THE PAGE ELEMENTS, INPUT TEXT OR PLACE NAVIGATIONAL ELEMENTS, HTML CODE IS BEING WRITTEN.

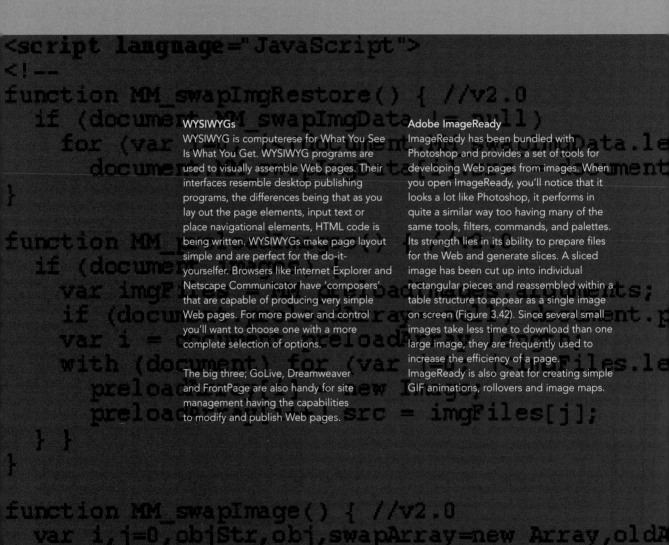

WYSIWYGs

WYSIWYG is computerese for What You See Is What You Get. WYSIWYG programs are used to visually assemble Web pages. Their interfaces resemble desktop publishing programs, the differences being that as you lay out the page elements, input text or place navigational elements, HTML code is being written. WYSIWYGs make page layout simple and are perfect for the do-it-yourselfer. Browsers like Internet Explorer and Netscape Communicator have 'composers' that are capable of producing very simple Web pages. For more power and control you'll want to choose one with a more complete selection of options.

The big three; GoLive, Dreamweaver and FrontPage are also handy for site management having the capabilities to modify and publish Web pages.

Adobe ImageReady

ImageReady has been bundled with Photoshop and provides a set of tools for developing Web pages from images. When you open ImageReady, you'll notice that it looks a lot like Photoshop, it performs in quite a similar way too having many of the same tools, filters, commands, and palettes. Its strength lies in its ability to prepare files for the Web and generate slices. A sliced image has been cut up into individual rectangular pieces and reassembled within a table structure to appear as a single image on screen (Figure 3.42). Since several small images take less time to download than one large image, they are frequently used to increase the efficiency of a page. ImageReady is also great for creating simple GIF animations, rollovers and image maps.

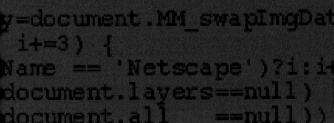

```
h-1);  i+=2)
_swapImgData[i+1];




oadArray = new Array();


h; j++) if (imgFiles[j].




y=document.MM_swapImgDat
 i+=3) {
Name == 'Netscape')?i:i-
document.layers==null)
document.all   ==null))
```

Figure 3.41
The Adobe ImageReady splash screen.

Figure 3.42
An image sliced in ImageReady.

Figure 3.43
Photoshop's Web Photo Gallery feature.

Adobe Photoshop

Want an instant, no fuss, no muss Web portfolio? Once you have chosen a series of images for presentation and placed them in a folder, you can quickly publish them to a digital portfolio by using Photoshop's Web Photo Gallery feature. You will be given a number of choices, including 11 layout styles, and easy-to-select image size and colour combinations. Once you have made those choices, press OK, and Photoshop does the rest for you, churning out Web-ready HTML documents. If you don't like your layout, go back to the Web Photo Gallery and experiment with the options. You can soon tailor your pages to show off your images to their best advantage.

This feature produces a Web portfolio practically instantaneously with a minimum of effort and with enough customisable features to produce a site that is interesting and attractive. Bear in mind however, that it doesn't offer the same custom options as the other WYSIWYG programs.

Macromedia Fireworks

Macromedia's basic image editing and Web authoring program, Fireworks, offers a different approach to Web authoring. The advantage of Fireworks is that like Adobe Illustrator or Macromedia Freehand, it is primarily vector based rather than pixel based. When you build a Web page in Fireworks you are building individual objects using Bezier curves instead of pixels.

Photoshop and ImageReady utilise pixels to create images. Fireworks is designed to produce Web elements with the flexibility and control of Illustrator and Freehand. Fireworks also has storyboarding, interactivity, animation and optimisation capabilities. In addition, you can import raster images and publish your documents directly from the program.

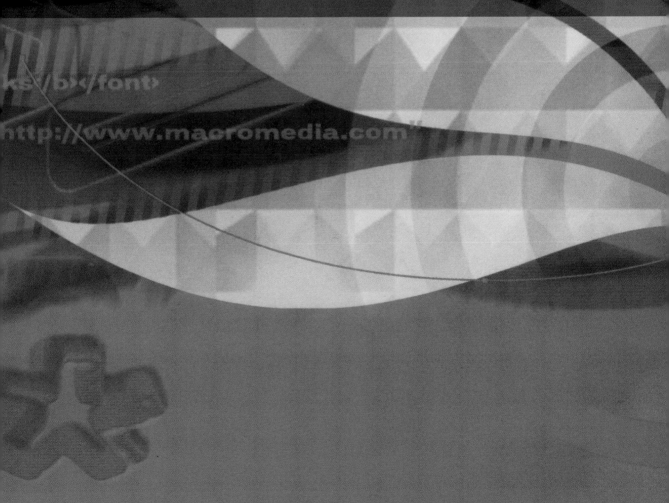

Figure 3.44
Fireworks splash screen.

Figure 3.45
Multimedia elements in www.geoffgourley.com.

Figure 3.46
Multimedia elements in www.dumdum.co.uk

The Big WYSIWYGs

Adobe GoLive
Macromedia Dreamweaver
Microsoft FrontPage

These three programs are the mainstays of Web publishing. They all resemble each other in that they share comprehensive Web authoring capabilities. Each has the capacity to create, publish and manage complete websites. All share features like a layout surface, in which Web elements can be positioned and scaled. All can generate Web pages in a layout mode that behaves very much like a desktop publishing program, or directly in HTML, which allows you to generate and edit code. All have a preview mode that enables you to see the page in the browser of your choice. They also have Web tools that are capable of creating static, interactive, or multimedia page elements.

The three programs do of course vary in their interfaces, but in general they have the same capabilities. The one you choose will depend on your personal preferences. There are differences of course, for example, FrontPage provides templates and wizards that make it easy to get started and has an interface similar to other Microsoft Office products, where as GoLive is very strong in site management and multimedia, and Dreamweaver interfaces superbly with other Macromedia products like Fireworks and Flash. However, if you're stumped as to which one to purchase you can download preview versions of the software at www.adobe.com, www.macromedia.com, or www.microsoft.com.

Multimedia

Multimedia is a very broad-based term used to describe the practice of combining elements from different artistic or communication media. The digital revolution has spawned a new medium, allowing individuals or small teams with limited resources access to exciting graphic, animation and audio tools and the means of reaching a worldwide audience. Recent and constantly improving software place the use of digital video sequences, 'flipbook' style animations (GIFs), image mapping (where portions of a graphic page are 'mapped' to lead to a new HTML page with a cursor click) and rollovers, in which an image changes or becomes animated when a cursor 'moves' over it, in the hands of the user. The extent to which you choose to utilise these features will depend upon a number of factors. As a Web designer, your client might expect you to create a multimedia *tour de force* from the beginning, using all the tools at your disposal to create an engaging website.

For the artist creating a digital portfolio with the primary focus on photography or illustration, a little boost from the multimedia vocabulary can help lift your presentation to new levels, perhaps transforming a mundane 'slide show' into a dynamic visual showcase without detracting from your primary goal, *getting your work noticed*. Which options you choose will depend, of course, on the nature of your own work, tastes and preferences as well as the time and budget you are willing to commit to your digital portfolio. For example,

photographer Geoff Gourley's home page, www.geoffgourley.com, is spare and uncluttered and features a single black-and-white image. Roll over the picture with the cursor, however, and suddenly the photo changes to full colour, instantly grabbing your attention and pulling you into the site (Figure 3.45). The design firm dumdum (www.dumdum.co.uk) takes a very high end approach, using Macromedia Flash sound and animation sequences to create a home page with all the flair of the opening credits to a feature film, as a means of introducing its impressive commercial portfolio (Figure 3.46).

Even if your digital portfolio isn't aimed at the Internet audience, there are many ways the new technologies can be useful. You might consider including a QuickTime Movie introduction to your work on a CD-ROM in addition to a traditional cover letter, or a voiceover commentary on your work in lieu of captioning.

Whether you choose to 'keep it simple' and just use dissolves to smooth the transitions between your portfolio images, or feel that presentation is everything and go to great lengths to create an exciting audiovisual display of your work, you can enhance the chances of catching the attention of a potential client with a multimedia trick or two.

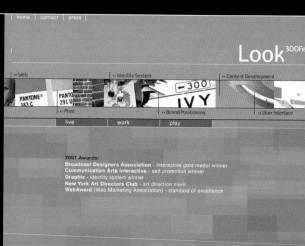

Figure 3.47
The Macromedia Flash splash screen.

Figure 3.48
300 Feet Out Flash website, www.300feetout.com.

Macromedia Flash & Adobe LiveMotion

These two cutting-edge full-tilt Web multimedia programs include many features for combining slides, movies, animation, sound and illustration, to make your portfolio into a complete multimedia extravaganza. Both are very powerful programs with many features that include motion animated text generation, vector-based content, interactive streaming video, image animation, audio, bitmap graphics and superb interactivity.

Websites generated in Flash or LiveMotion require Flash Player to run them, which can be acquired by clicking on a link on the site or at www.macromedia.com.

Let's go straight to the Web and find some examples of the way Flash can be used, either to show off Flash expertise, or to enhance but not overpower your photo or illustration portfolio. A site that uses a relatively simple, easy-to-view technique is www.300feetout.com (Figure 3.48). Here, a horizontal banner screen presents a variety of images representative of the firm's work. Centring the mouse halts the moving screen, and moving the mouse left or right scrolls the screen in that direction at an accelerating pace. This eye catcher then gives way to a more muted, traditional site with easy-to-use menu and button navigation and strong, stand-alone illustration windows.

re 3.49
otle use of multimedia graphics and sound, www.estelleklawitter.de.

A photography site that uses a very different approach is www.estelleklawitter.de (Figure 3.49). Here, the word subtlety describes this interesting use of high-end multimedia graphics and sound.

For those of you who feel a rather simple Flash routine might give some punch to your Web portfolio but are not ready for highly sophisticated Web design, yet don't feel that hiring a Web designer is feasible or desirable, Flash offers a variety of easy-to-use templates which can get you on the Web in a hurry. You might find that you can get a better template going this route than using Adobe Photoshop's Web Gallery or Extensis Portfolio's Save for Web features. You will have gained some Flash experience, and you will be putting together the building blocks for a more sophisticated Flash site. In addition to its templates, Flash does offer excellent on-screen lessons and tutorial guides, making building a site element by element a rewarding, self-paced experience.

Figure 3.50
An email 'form letter' at www.maxhampel.com.

Figure 3.51
An easy-to-locate response form at
www.jimmykatz.com.

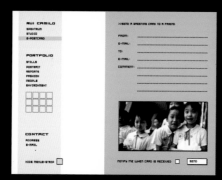

Figure 3.52
An e-postcard at www.rui-camilo.de.

Response Forms

To a large degree, your very reasons for putting together a digital portfolio will determine the manner in which you seek responses from your viewers. Almost mandatory, of course, is a contact page. Here, while a mailing address and/or phone number are important, an email address may be the most important. People finding you on the Web are likely to wish to respond via the Web. Many successful sites include an email 'form letter' to nudge interested parties a little closer to making contact (Figure 3.50).

If you are creating a website with the intention of making direct sales to the public, like www.jimmykatz.com (Figure 3.51), creating an easy-to-locate response form is as important as the work you showcase. In this case a simple pricing schedule and mail-to form are included in the site. If you are a fine artist or photographer whose works aren't satisfyingly presented by virtue of scale or colour limitations on the Web, your digital portfolio is probably only being used as a teaser to induce potential buyers to take a closer look at your work, but this needn't eliminate making a direct sales offering. A creative way of gauging interest in your site, while 'spreading the word' about it is to offer an e-postcard. As in www.rui-camilo.de this response form has a little more punch and has the advantage of being a practical application of the photographer's work. It also offers 'something for nothing' (you can send this postcard to anyone) while communicating the scope of the photographer's talents (Figure 3.52).

E_MAIL

Advertising

All of the methods mentioned above are, directly or indirectly, a form of advertising, but fresh exposure to your work needn't stop at your website or be confined to a CD-ROM.

Links are one example. While it is good Internet etiquette not to provide links to others' websites without their knowledge or permission, it is good business practice to network with other artists on the Web with whom you share some common interest. By trading links, you can both increase the size of the audience for your work and experience the synergistic rewards of working within a larger artists' community. Another way of realising some trade-off value is the use of banner ads. These 'digital billboards' can be used in several ways. It might be profitable for you to advertise on other carefully selected websites, or you might consider carrying an ad on your site to help offset the costs of your Web presence. In either case, there are clearinghouse firms that can help you choose the type of arrangements that might be beneficial to you.

The multimedia revolution and the Internet have transformed some more traditional ways of seeking business as well. Perhaps a kiosk showing a video of you at work in your studio will draw people into your booth at an art or crafts fair. Also, in many public places display racks are appearing offering free postcards carrying advertising for local businesses. Placing a printed card of one of your images in one of these venues is an excellent way of finding new customers. And, of course, now that you've decided to go digital with your portfolio, encourage people to seek it out by including your new Web address on your business card and other printed materials.

Figure 3.53
Adobe GoLive's FTP feature.

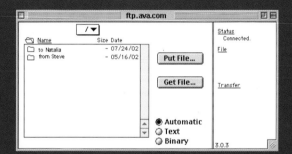

Figure 3.54
The Fetch FTP interface.

Publishing Your Portfolio

Once you've built the Web portfolio using some of the extraordinary tools discussed in this section, the next step is to publish it. This process involves choosing a name for the site. A variety of services exist for registering a site name and they usually charge a yearly fee.

Among some of the thousands of domain registration sites is the following list. Compare services and pricing. Or run a search for domain registration in any one of the popular search engines.

Name	URL
Buy Domain.com	www.buydomain.com
DotYou.com	www.DotYou.com
Moonlight computing	www.mooncomp.com
Access Internet	www.Access-inter.net
Access One	www.accessone.net
Parichaya.com	www.parichaya.com
Front Host.net	www.fronthost.net

Once you have a site domain registered, you will contact a service provider who will give you a password to an FTP (File Transfer Protocol) site. You'll upload your files to the server. The Big WYSIWYG programs all offer FTP publishing capabilities (Figure 3.53), or you might use a program like Fetch (Figure 3.54) to perform this task. When uploading files, it's crucial that they remain in the same folders as they are on your computer in order to be read by the browser. In that the HTML code, written by hand or in the WYSIWYG programs reflects their position in the file hierarchy.

04 **PEOPLE**

YOUR PORTFOLIO MUST BE A SHINING EXAMPLE OF THE EXTENT
OF YOUR TALENT.

Your portfolio is designed to communicate. No matter how you approach the presentation
of your work, no matter how many cool multimedia effects and Flash animations your
portfolio contains, if it doesn't directly and honestly present your talents to the world, it has
failed in its mission.

The ultimate choice of who hires you depends of course on the sensibilities of your client.
Your efforts to reach your prospective client must be focused on educating and enlightening
them to your capabilities. Your portfolio must be a shining example of the extent of your
talent. The client will be looking at your work to determine whether you fit into his or her
niche. No doubt, questions like these will be going through his or her mind: Is your style
appropriate for the particular job? Do you have the experience to adapt your skills to the
task at hand? Can you expedite the task in a professional and timely manner? By its
aesthetic qualities, look and feel and of course its content, your portfolio should be able to
answer these questions.

Figure 4.0
Image taken from www.marlaart.com.

As a graphics professional, you are working in an extremely competitive market. There is a lot of incredible talent out there as you will see in the next pages. The owners of these portfolios are some of the best in the business and with their kind permission, I proudly show their portfolios here in order for you to see the amazing variety and creativity that can potentially go into a digital portfolio. No two are alike, and the design, the interactivity and the images they display in all cases reflect the scope of the artist's work and their individual personalities. These portfolios are calculated to make an impression and invoke a response from the viewer.

With each portfolio I have included an interview, which will help you to better get to know the artists and the scope of their work. I present a few screen shots on each page to give you an idea of their accomplishments. But to get a more comprehensive impression of their abilities, I encourage you to log on to their websites and spend some time looking around. You can easily access links to their sites by visiting The Perfect Digital Portfolio website at www.avabooks.ch/avaguides/digitalportfolio/. I hope you will come away from the experience inspired by a new sense of the potential of this dynamic new medium.

Marla has been illustrating for 19 years with breaks to have and raise kids! Her portfolio has been on-line for three years.

Artist's Statement:
I love to do whimsical work with a sense of mystery and wonder. I enjoy doing children's illustration because kids are a great audience and are receptive to a wide range of imagery.

 How many hits on the site do you get per week?
I don't know, but I've been really busy and people are going to my site.

 On a scale of 1 to 10, how would you rate its effectiveness in obtaining clients?
It has been an extremely effective tool. Prospective clients can view my entire portfolio on-line with great ease. Rather than go through the hassle of sending my portfolio overnight to be in the running for a job, clients can look at a whole body of my work without ever having to contact me. By the time I get a call, they have usually already decided that they'd like to use me for the job.

 How do you distribute information about where to access your portfolio?
I advertise in source books; Blackbook, Picturebook and Workbook. I also do direct mail. I hope there is some word of mouth!

 Did you work with a Web designer to create the website? If so, who was the designer?
I am very fortunate to have a husband who is a great designer. He and I designed the site. His name is Mike Baggetta. His company is Baggetta & Associates. He used Photoshop and Adobe GoLive.

 Do you have a CD or disk version of the portfolio that you distribute?
I haven't sent out a disk version yet. Luckily, I've been too busy.

Anna has been illustrating for two years. Her portfolio has been on-line since December 2000.

Artist's Statement:
I work mainly in paint to illustrate ideas and narratives in a way that can express an emotional and psychological depth.

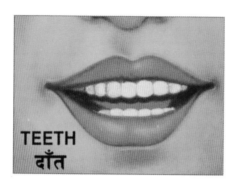

How many hits on the site do you get per week?
Average 737.

On a scale of 1 to 10, how would you rate its effectiveness in obtaining clients?
Five.

How do you distribute information about where to access your portfolio?
Word of mouth and links from other sites like Association of Illustrators, mail shots, catalogues – Images 26.

Did you work with a Web designer to create the website? If so, who was the designer?
I designed it myself using Adobe GoLive, ImageReady and Photoshop.

Do you have a CD or disk version of the portfolio that you distribute?
No.

Amanda has been in business since 1989, but mostly as a prop-maker. The portraiture slips in between. Her portfolio has been on-line for about a year.

Artist's Statement:
I became tired of painting grinning children in their Sunday best and decided to attract a new type of client, one with a spirit of adventure (or just 'spirit' will do!). As a prop-maker, making things look hundreds of years old has become second nature, and my portraits are no exception. I'm mesmerised by Renaissance portraits, so I want to evoke the same sense of mystery in my own work.

How many hits on the site do you get per week?
I don't have a counter. Gotta get me one of those!

On a scale of 1 to 10, how would you rate its effectiveness in obtaining clients?
Three, but its primary goal is not to obtain clients but to have an on-line presence and not have to lug my portfolio around so much.

How do you distribute information about where to access your portfolio?
Posters, business cards, emails and word of mouth.

Did you work with a Web designer to create the website? If so, who was the designer?
I designed it and my partner built it. He used Dreamweaver and Fireworks.

Do you have a CD or disk version of the portfolio that you distribute?
No. If a potential client asks to see more work I email it.

Cyrus has been illustrating full time for the past four years and part time for six years. His website went on-line in February 2002.

Artist's Statement:
I provide a professional illustration service for editorial, publishing, design and advertising clients. My work varies from simple icons to large complex images. Using a black line and flat colour, the whole process is rendered digitally in Illustrator 8. My work also benefits from clever ideas, which is important as this helps me to stand out from the huge crowd of illustrators. I email the final artwork, which is an advantage with tight deadlines. My speed of work also has clients commissioning me for the quick turn around.

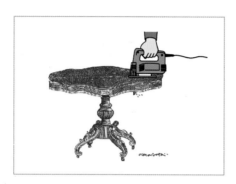
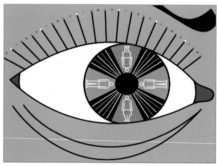

How many hits on the site do you get per week?
Current hits per month are approximately 10,000.

On a scale of 1 to 10, how would you rate its effectiveness in obtaining clients?
Seven out of ten. It's great to have an on-line portfolio. Clients have checked my work on-line before contacting me. When I am extremely busy, and cannot make a portfolio meeting or drop off, I ask if they have visited my website and direct them to it. Clients appreciate you having an on-line portfolio that they can refer to at any time.

How do you distribute information about where to access your portfolio?
I print the URL of my website on all my stationery. Major updates to the site are followed by direct mail shots to clients. This is effective, as I see my hits for that month rise steeply in which the mailers were sent. I inform clients at the end of a meeting that my work can be viewed on-line, and a new image is posted every two weeks under the 'Latest Image' link. I also advertise in source books such as Contact 18 and Images 26, where my URL is included in the contact details.

Did you work with a Web designer to create the website? If so, who was the designer?
I created the website myself. I attended an HTML course and learned how to write code for the Mac system. I do not use a Web design program. It was money well spent.

Do you have a CD or disk version of the portfolio that you distribute?
I do not have a portfolio on disk. I feel that the on-line portfolio is efficient, along with the more traditional printed business cards I send out.

Joe has been in business for 22 years, his website has been on-line for two years.

Artist's Statement:

Before I went quietly mad I quit working as a producer for a large London Internet design operation. And I returned to my first love, no not her, but illustration. But all those years of pixel bashing were not totally wasted. I was able to build my own site and show all those pieces, new and old, that had sat festering in my portfolio / hard drive for years.

I now work in a variety of illustrative styles. The great thing about the website is the viewer can search for examples of just digital vector-based images (or oil based, or animation or by content etc.). It's great, as a new piece is produced it can be added to the site (the printed brochure was so out of date by the time it was delivered). I've also set a preview area on the back of the website where clients can see work in progress.

 How many hits on the site do you get per week?
Approximately 60.

 On a scale of 1 to 10, how would you rate its effectiveness in obtaining clients?
I'd rate it an eight. The site reaches places I couldn't think of reaching – I'm currently talking to a specialist publisher in Dallas. I can't remember the last time I had to drag the vinyl portfolio around London; I just give ADs the URL.

 Did you work with a Web designer to create the website? If so, who was the designer?
I created the site using Dreamweaver, Photoshop, Fetch and Illustrator.

 Do you have a CD or disk version of the portfolio that you distribute?
I don't have a disk of the site.

Ramon has been illustrating for six years. His portfolio has been on-line for three years.

Artist's Statement:
My work (and website) is an exercise in trying to simplify an image to its most basic form – black shapes with colour in the negative space. I feel that if done well, the image can be quite powerful, and I enjoy working with subject matter that lends itself to that kind of powerful image. Thus, I'm a big fan of high contrast work like Michael Schwab or Christopher Wormell.

 How many hits on the site do you get per week?
I quite honestly don't track the number of hits.

 On a scale of 1 to 10, how would you rate its effectiveness in obtaining clients?
The website seldom gets me new clients by itself, as much as it clinches the sale with clients I have already contacted by other means, or clients who have received my mailers or seen my directory ad.

 How do you distribute information about where to access your portfolio?
I have a page in the Directory of Illustration and I send out a direct mail piece two to three times a year. Plus I try to get my site listed on as many search engines and directories and listings as possible.

 Did you work with a Web designer to create the website? If so, who was the designer?
I designed the site myself. I kept the layout simple to allow fast access to the work and I used ImageReady and hand coded the HTML. I refrained from using Frames or Flash or anything that might prevent a viewer from seeing the site. The portfolio is centred both horizontally and vertically so that the layout works with any size of browser window.

 Do you have a CD or disk version of the portfolio that you distribute?
Yes.

Rich Grote

Freelance Illustration – www.rgrote.com

Richard has been illustrating for 27 years. His portfolio has been on-line for seven years.

Artist's Statement:
I've done most of my work for the New York market but have been published worldwide. I've worked on book jackets, magazine covers and inside illustrations and many different types of print advertising.

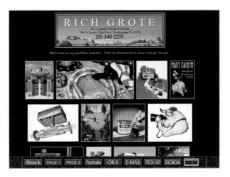

How many hits on the site do you get per week?
I'm not sure since that's not the focus of my site. I use it as a portfolio and direct prospective clients to it. I don't do anything to encourage random Web browsers. In the last two years I've used www.portfolios.com as a second site that leads to my site for that purpose.

On a scale of 1 to 10, how would you rate its effectiveness in obtaining clients?
I would rate it as a ten, but only as a part of a total sales strategy.

How do you distribute information about where to access your portfolio?
My website URL is printed on all of my print promotional material LARGE. I send out HTML emails with an example image that's linked to my website. (I have an email list of past and prospective clients.)

Did you work with a Web designer to create the website? If so, who was the designer?
I did it myself with FrontPage and Dreamweaver.

Do you have a CD or disk version of the portfolio that you distribute?
Not an HTML version, I just use a CD with JPEG files that people can browse.

Cheryl has been working professionally since 1994 when she graduated with a design degree. She did freelance work on evenings/weekends in addition to her day job as an art director/graphic designer until she became independent one and a half years ago. She has been illustrating for three years. Her portfolio has been on-line for three years.

Artist's Statement:

I generally try to illustrate what I like...fashion, beauty, travel, decor, music, spa and other such lifestyle situations. I also enjoy portraits. My primary influence is magazines: fashion, travel and decor. I typically illustrate something for myself because I'm interested in exploring it. Then, once it is in my portfolio, I get calls to do a similar project. In addition to liking your style, people like to see that you have specifically handled their subject matter before they hire you.

How many hits on the site do you get per week?

I don't track that. Even if I did, I probably wouldn't look at it. What I focus on is how many and what type of clients I am getting. I always ask them how they came across my work.

On a scale of 1 to 10, how would you rate its effectiveness in obtaining clients?

I don't think it finds the clients, as in traditional marketing, but I think it closes the deal. Having my portfolio posted on-line makes my life a million times easier than shipping an actual portfolio all over the country and getting new work professionally mounted. I've done that, it's brutal. In addition, I tend to worry about which pieces of work to send to a prospective client. I haven't really had to worry about that with my portfolio on the Web. People who come across my work on-line have already looked at my website and found what they wanted to see by the time they contact me.

How do you distribute information about where to access your portfolio?

I currently pay to have 20 images posted on www.portfolios.com which is where most of my clients have found me. I intend to purchase space on a few other such websites as I can afford to spend more money on marketing. I also carry business cards with my website address.

Did you work with a Web designer to create the website? If so, who was the designer?

I created my site by teaching myself to use Macromedia products – Dreamweaver to build the site and Fireworks to crop and optimise images. I found their tutorials to be very user-friendly. Originally, my website had been more complexly designed, but the more I mess with it the simpler it gets. It's never finished, always changing with my whims.

Do you have a CD or disk version of the portfolio that you distribute?

No. I am experimenting with HTML email, which means when the recipient receives my message in their email, it's very graphic looking like a Web page with linked images to my site. This is a lot less expensive than mailing printed postcards.

Matt has been illustrating for four years. His portfolio has been on-line for three years.

Artist's Statement:
Most of my commissions have come from editorial and publishing clients. My work is mostly figurative and I am generally commissioned to illustrate human interest articles or work on more literary or arts-based projects.

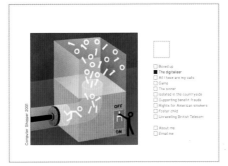

On a scale of 1 to 10, how would you rate its effectiveness in obtaining clients?
I'd rate it at seven. I use the website only in conjunction with other promotions like direct mail.

How do you distribute information about where to access your portfolio?
Through direct mail.

Did you work with a Web designer to create the website? If so, who was the designer?
I created the site using Fireworks, Dreamweaver and Photoshop.

Do you have a CD or disk version of the portfolio that you distribute?
I don't use any additional media.

Ken has been a digital artist for four years. His portfolio has been on-line for three years.

Artist's Statement:
I create digital illustration and design for editorial and corporate print, I also do animations and Web design.

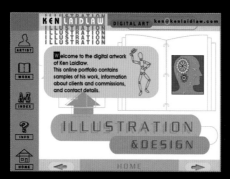
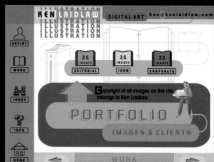

 How many hits on the site do you get per week?
Usually 1000–2000.

 On a scale of 1 to 10, how would you rate its effectiveness in obtaining clients?
Seven.

 How do you distribute information about where to access your portfolio?
Direct mail flyers, correspondence (invoices, envelopes etc.), word of mouth.

 Did you work with a Web designer to create the website? If so, who was the designer?
I designed it myself using Photoshop, Illustrator, GoLive, ImageReady, ImageStyler, GifBuilder, MS Explorer and Netscape Navigator.

 Do you have a CD or disk version of the portfolio that you distribute?
Yes, I distribute the portfolio on hard media.

*Paul has been illustrating for eight years.
His portfolio has been on-line for two and a
half years.*

Artist's Statement:
My work is mainly doing design and
illustration work in the fields of fashion
(mainly T-shirt graphics), music (album
covers) and films (titles, art direction). But
generally most things that require throwing
some ideas together.

How many hits on the site do you get per week?
About 800.

On a scale of 1 to 10, how would you rate its effectiveness in obtaining clients?
I'd rate it six. Well, I'm not positive that it's directly got me one serious job. The good jobs
I have got have been through art directors seeing my work printed in books! Presumably
people have looked at my site before deciding to use me. I think a lot of traffic comes from
inquisitive kids, they give me the feedback and admiration and I'm happy that kids enjoy it and
want to forge their own careers from seeing my work. That said, I have a printed portfolio and
there's no way I could have shown that to the thousands of people who have visited my site!
So as far as reaching people, yes it's effective, but job-wise I'm not so sure.

How do you distribute information about where to access your portfolio?
Links to other sites and business cards. Initially I emailed a flyer to a list of about 250 dream
clients. But now it's word of mouth.

Did you work with a Web designer to create the website? If so, who was the designer?
I designed the site in Freehand and used a Flash technician to put the puppy together; his
name is Brendan Cook.

Do you have a CD or disk version of the portfolio that you distribute?
No, I feel that would be overdoing it, I mean if someone has the technology to look at a disk
then presumably they can look at the Web. If they haven't got the time to do that, then cripes
I'm not sure if I want to work with someone that impatient.

Arthur has been in the business for six years. His portfolio has been on-line for three years.

Artist's Statement:
Digital vector-based illustration! I like to keep things simple, simple shapes and nice flat colours. My work is fairly solemn in tone; I'm not too flashy. I'm drawn to architecture, fashion, portraits and travel. I've done work for clients in a very wide range of industries. I really enjoy what I do and think I'm pretty good at it.

 How many hits on the site do you get per week?
I don't know, I'd says hundreds judging by the amount of fan email I receive.

 On a scale of 1 to 10, how would you rate its effectiveness in obtaining clients?
I'd rate it eight.

 How do you distribute information about where to access your portfolio?
Direct mail (postcards), email, word of mouth, client referrals. Lots of people find my site through various link sites and design portals.

 Did you work with a Web designer to create the website? If so, who was the designer?
I designed, built, and maintain it myself. I used Flash and Illustrator.

 Do you have a CD or disk version of the portfolio that you distribute?
Not yet, I'll probably have one before too long.

Bud has been working as a designer and illustrator since 1986, and has been on-line since 1996.

Artist's Statement:

I am primarily an editorial illustrator who has expanded over the years into many areas. I've always thought of myself as a colourist and, due to my extensive training as a sculptor, always try to infuse movement in all my work. I consider myself a problem solver and many clients come to me with unusual projects that need an unusual solution. These projects consist of such assignments as designing animations for cell phone LCD screens; building a computerised 3D forest for the National Geographic website; designing surface art for books and journals; illustrating interactive art for corporate websites; designing furniture ensembles and accessories; and building sculptural 3D sets.

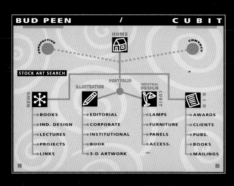
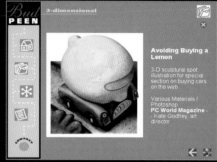

 How many hits on the site do you get per week?
Hard to say. Around 300–600 per week.

 On a scale of 1 to 10, how would you rate its effectiveness in obtaining clients?
Ten. I think a website is crucial to promoting your work. Clients don't ask for portfolios anymore: they just want your Web address.

 How do you distribute information about where to access your portfolio?
I use direct mail, workbooks (American Showcase, Workbook), email notices, and other artist's links.

 Did you work with a Web designer to create the website? If so, who was the designer?
I designed and produced it myself, using Adobe's GoLive.

 Do you have a CD or disk version of the portfolio that you distribute?
I do not have a CD version, although on some occasions I've put one together on the fly for a particular project. I've also uploaded to my site a group of illustrations for a particular client or project.

Dave has been in business for 18 years, Annie for 24. They have been on-line since 1996.

Artists' Statement:
We create images and animations for editorial, advertising and corporate clients, both in the US (where we're based) and abroad. While we maintain relationships with separate clients, as a married couple we find it fun to feature our work under one website. Clients who have worked with us separately are surprised when they visit our site to find that we're married. Frequently we find that visitors to the site who went specifically to look at Annie's work will check out Dave's as well, and vice versa.

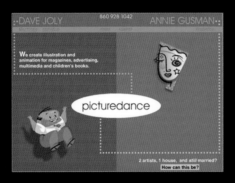

How many hits on the site do you get per week?
Approximately 500.

On a scale of 1 to 10, how would you rate its effectiveness in obtaining clients?
Seven in terms of generating jobs from a cold starting point, but ten in terms of creating greater interest in our work from existing and potential clients who we direct mail to.

How do you distribute information about where to access your portfolio?
Direct mail, targeted email (not spam) to existing clients, printed illustration directories, on-line directories.

Did you work with a Web designer to create the website? If so, who was the designer?
Dave creates and maintains the site. Dave started with hand-coding HTML, and then progressed through Adobe Pagemill, then to Adobe GoLive (because it came bundled with his laptop).

Do you have a CD or disk version of the portfolio that you distribute?
Periodically over the years we've created disk-based portfolios using Macromedia Director and Flash.

William Rieser

R2Design – www.r2design.com

William has been in business since 1979. His portfolio has been on-line for three years.

Artist's Statement:
Graphic illustration is the general area R2 has been operating in for the past 20 or so years. Packaging, point-of-purchase display, business systems, identities, and illustration as it relates to the previous areas.

How many hits on the site do you get per week?
I don't know.

On a scale of 1 to 10, how would you rate its effectiveness in obtaining clients?
Five.

How do you distribute information about where to access your portfolio?
Direct mail, word of mouth, advertising on other sites, and advertising in Blackbook, Directory of illustrators and similar publications.

Did you work with a Web designer to create the website? If so, who was the designer?
I designed the site, someone else built it.

Do you have a CD or disk version of the portfolio that you distribute?
Yes and I send out my portfolio as a PDF.

It's been six years since Erin graduated from Art School, and she's been very active with applying herself towards any and every freelance opportunity she can. In this way she has been able to work herself up the ladder, developing quite an extensive client list that continues to grow. Erin has been on-line for one year.

Artist's Statement:

I've been doing what I do since I was four years old and my genuine love of art continues as I discover new and exciting ways to express my visions. I enjoy creating projects from many vantage points, with the ability to not only conceptualise, but to also execute the sketches, illustrations, graphic design and whatever else is needed to ensure my clients the end product will exceed their expectations. This allows me to tap every resource in becoming the most well-rounded artist I can be. It's gratifying to know that what I created has helped many people, whether it's assisting with client's production or sales, or graphics general consumers can relate to. All of the hard work involved doesn't really seem like work if you love what you do!

Personally, I have many interests as to which direction my art could go. Some of my focuses have been to gain exposure in the entertainment industry (i.e. CD cover design, fashion illustrations, package design, movie posters, etc.), as well as magazines and other editorial spots. I love travel (hopefully to Europe soon), music, nostalgia, movies, fashion and much more – these areas continue to be my life's ambition.

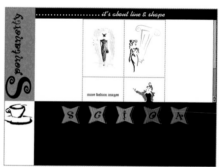

How many hits on the site do you get per week?
Approximately 100. I've recently changed hosts for my site – the new one provides a hidden tracker report from which I'll have a more accurate reading shortly. My 'guess-timate' is based on the number of website promo cards I send out on a weekly basis plus the number of responses I continue to receive regarding possible freelance work.

On a scale of 1 to 10, how would you rate its effectiveness in obtaining clients?
Eight.

How do you distribute information about where to access your portfolio?
For the past couple of years I've been creating self-promotion postcards to send as direct mail flyers.

Graphic Designers
While the consistency of style is of more importance in an illustrator's or photographer's portfolio, variety and flexibility might better debut a designer's talents. The ability to adapt idiom and style to a particular assignment while maintaining a consistent signature exemplifies the designer's skill. In the portfolios that follow, you will see the work of some of the world's best graphic designers who transform text, images and graphic elements into extraordinary communication tools that speak to the viewer.

TYPEDIFFERENT.COM
BD NIPPORI FONT
NISHI–NIPPORI

Chris first put his portfolio on-line in 1995. Cabedge.com has been on-line since 1999.

Artist's Statement:
I prefer to focus on Web design although I do quite a bit of 'identity' work along the way, (logos, letterheads and business cards).

Branding is very important to me. Whether inventing, enhancing, or reinforcing, I think it is important for a company to be consistent in its presentation. Not stopping at just visual design, I try to consult in all areas of brand when applicable. To me, brand is an overall voice, personality, or tone of a campaign.

 How many hits on the site do you get per week?
It varies. Some weekends are slow, while others peak. One day last summer, I had almost 1000 unique visitors in one day, while other days traffic hovered in the 500–700 per day range. According to the stats, July had an average of 451 unique visitors per day.

 On a scale of 1 to 10, how would you rate its effectiveness in obtaining clients?
It doesn't necessarily do all of the work. I think people hear about me one of a few different ways… 1) They see my site on-line and call me. 2) They hear about me from a mutual acquaintance, and then look at my site before calling me. 3) I meet them and refer them to my site. After taking a look, they give me a call. I think a designer's work should speak for itself in most cases, but when someone hires a designer, they should think of this new vendor as a 'partner' in helping them find a branding solution that works best for them and their company. Taken in this context, I think cabedge.com ranks an eight or nine with room for improvement.

 How do you distribute information about where to access your portfolio?
Word of mouth mostly. I don't do any other real advertising or cold calling.

 Did you work with a Web designer to create the website? If so, who was the designer?
I am the designer. I used Flash, Dreamweaver, Fireworks, and Photoshop running on a Mac (OS9 at first, then OSX for about the last five months).

 Do you have a CD or disk version of the portfolio that you distribute?
No. I don't see the point. You can do just about everything (if not more) on the Web as you can on a CD. In fact, I think it is much more accessible via the Web. If you want to share something with a colleague, there's no need to pop the disk out and walk/mail it to that colleague. Just shoot them a URL. With more and more people getting higher bandwidth connections, sharing files, sites, and ideas is becoming much easier.

Keith Pizer, Tom Romer, Matthew Richmond, Rob Reed

The Chopping Block, Inc. – www.choppingblock.com

'The Chopping Block was established in 1996 as a collective of Cooper Union graduates with a common desire for world domination through graphic design. Total world domination has yet to be achieved but the result over the past six years has gotten us much closer as we have overseen the creation of unique, quality graphic design projects. As a brand ourselves, we have successfully developed our own Block style and way of doing things. We have established our company personality through our client work and our own promotional materials. We have created various themed websites over the years from NASCAR, NASA, Horror, Cub Scouts, to our current Orange Farmers website. We have recently reinvented ourselves as Olympic Athletes to showcase our abilities in our new print media kit.' The Chopping Block has been on-line since its inception.

Artists' Statement:
We describe ourselves as a full-service graphic design studio founded on the principle that good design spans all media. Whether we are working on a website, kiosk application, book cover or print design we are constantly looking for new ways to communicate ideas to the masses. When asked how we go about creating our websites, we often say that the first step is to think how we can make the website not look like a website. It is an ongoing challenge to find a new and better way to approach everything and we try to do this with our design.

Since we are a boutique and not an agency, we are able to move quickly and nimbly in an environment that demands flexibility. This unique position has allowed us to experiment with new technologies, develop a suite of customisable tools which help preserve the integrity of our design projects, and ultimately create consistent award-winning work.

 How many hits on the site do you get per week?
Not available at this time.

 On a scale of 1 to 10, how would you rate its effectiveness in obtaining clients?
Eight.

 How do you distribute information about where to access your portfolio?
Word of mouth and an opt-in email newsletter.

 Did you work with a Web designer to create the website? If so, who was the designer?
We created our website. We are currently working on a new incarnation. We developed the current site about two years ago, so we used Flash 4 at the time.

 Do you have a CD or disk version of the portfolio that you distribute?
We have a sampler CD that we distributed last year (so the jobs are not completely current). We also have a print media kit that we distribute to prospective clients.

Peter has been in business for two years. His portfolio has been on-line for 18 months.

Artist's Statement:
Our primary focus is print design, covering areas such as identity, literature, direct mail and publishing. Designs of websites are included in the portfolio, but due to our abilities in conceptual thinking and strong typographic skills we seem to mainly focus on print design.

 How many hits on the site do you get per week?
50–150.

 On a scale of 1 to 10, how would you rate its effectiveness in obtaining clients?
Six.

 How do you distribute information about where to access your portfolio?
I use direct mail and email.

 Did you work with a Web designer to create the website? If so, who was the designer?
No we designed it ourselves (Peter Dawson and Paul Palmer-Edwards). Andy Talbot programmed it. We used Photoshop, Illustrator and Flash.

 Do you also have a CD or disk version of the portfolio that you distribute?
No.

buro destruct has been in existence since 1992 and on-line since 1994.

Artist's Statement:
I want to keep buro destruct as an eerie feeling.

How many hits on the site do you get per week?
About 11,000.

On a scale of 1 to 10, how would you rate its effectiveness in obtaining clients?
We don't design our site with the main target being obtaining clients. Let's say five.

How do you distribute information about where to access your portfolio?
Our site automatically promotes itself with contributions from various design books, articles in magazines, through links from other sites, and by broadcasting our news at newstoday.com.

Did you work with a Web designer to create the website? If so, who was the designer?
We did it ourselves. We used Simple Text, Adobe GoLive and Macromedia Flash.

Do you have a CD or disk version of the portfolio that you distribute?
No.

Betsy has been in business for five years. Her portfolio has been on-line for five years.

Artist's Statement:
I am both an illustrator and a designer, and I try to give my attention to both equally. However, I find there to be a much higher demand for design, so I work a lot on that side. My goal in design is to provide a very clean, easy-to-look-at piece that also delivers all the necessary content. Form follows function. To that end, I try to find a flavour that is appropriate for the task at hand, a design direction that speaks for the company or product, and gives it personality, without needing words to explain it.

Web design is my favourite design medium. It is easy to produce and has potentially the widest audience. It is by far the most easily accessible. And it is virtually free. I can explore and go crazy, explode all over the place and then reel it back in. I can test it live and then take it down if I want to change it and I haven't committed to huge printing costs.

With illustration, I take a different direction. I see illustration as an opportunity to create a whole new world and exploit my artistic license. I love to bring joy to the eye, creating 'timeless' figures and environments when possible, bringing mood to the piece whether it be mellow or dynamic. However, I try to make those timeless figures and spaces as relevant and modern as possible. The feel is often both antiquated and current at the same time, and because of this it inherently creates a unique 'world'. People sometimes tell me that they wish they could go into my illustrations and be in those unique spaces. That makes me happy and I feel like I have accomplished what I had set out to do.

How many hits on the site do you get per week?
About 1,000.

On a scale of 1 to 10, how would you rate its effectiveness in obtaining clients?
For obtaining clients, as in the 'found me cold on the Web', three. That is probably due to my not advertising or putting forth effort to get my site at the top of the search engine results. As for retaining clients who were directed to it by an associate, or me I would say nine. I find that once people get to see all of my work on-line, they are impressed and want to work with me.

How do you distribute information about where to access your portfolio?
Word of mouth, then email.

Did you work with a Web designer to create the website? If so, who was the designer?
I was the sole designer and producer of my website. I created it in Flash 4, which I taught myself.

Do you have a CD or disk version of the portfolio that you distribute?
Yes. It's a copy of my website on a CD. I have plans to create a fresh look, other than my website, specifically for a showcase CD.

John Simpson

SEA Design – www.seadesign.co.uk

John has been working as a graphic designer for five years. His portfolio has been on-line for two years.

Artist's Statement:

To create original, relevant and memorable design solutions.

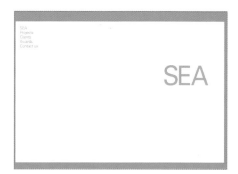

How many hits on the site do you get per week?
150 per week.

On a scale of 1 to 10, how would you rate its effectiveness in obtaining clients?
Seven.

How do you distribute information about where to access your portfolio?
Word of mouth and direct mail.

Did you work with a Web designer to create the website? If so, who was the designer?
We designed the site ourselves using HTML and Flash.

Do you have a CD or disk version of the portfolio that you distribute?
No.

Raphael has been in business since 1988. The first version of his Web portfolio was on-line in 1997.

Artist's statement:
After many years as a graphic designer for firms in France (1988–1993) and Germany (1993–present), I founded the etrema project in 2000. It is a graphic collaboration for design studios and multimedia agencies. I work especially on design for the music industry (CD covers), corporate design and multimedia design, and work directly as art director for music labels and music clubs.

How many hits on the site do you get per week?
Unknown at this time.

On a scale of 1 to 10, how would you rate its effectiveness in obtaining clients?
Five.

How do you distribute information about where to access your portfolio?
Flyers, direct mail (newsletter), usually people 'find' my portfolio through links on other pages.

Did you work with a Web designer to create the website? If so, who was the designer?
I designed it myself with Adobe GoLive.

Do you have a CD or disk version of the portfolio that you distribute?
Yes, I distribute a CD version when requested.

Hillman has been in business for four and a half years. And his site has been up and running since the inception.

Artist's Statement:

My work is new media design, which means it is generally aimed at, designed for, and eventually lives on the Web. This includes website design, motion design (Flash), interactive design, streaming video design and production. When I say new media design, I mean that the design encompasses both the visual as well as the functional.

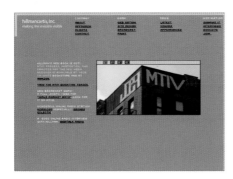 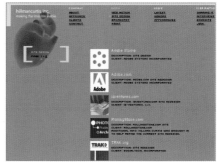

How many hits on the site do you get per week?

Somewhere around 50 to 100.

On a scale of 1 to 10, how would you rate its effectiveness in obtaining clients?

It's around a seven or an eight.

How do you distribute information about where to access your portfolio?

Most of the traffic comes from press, my books, links from other sites and very much word of mouth.

Did you work with a Web designer to create the website? If so, who was the designer?

No, it was all done by me using Macromedia Flash and Dreamweaver, Adobe Photoshop and ImageReady, and Final Cut Pro and Sorenson Squeeze.

Do you have a CD or disk version of the portfolio that you distribute?

No.

Photographers
The preponderance of digital portfolios
found on the Web belong to photographers.
The Web portfolio is the fastest and simplest
way to post the most recent images and to
communicate directly with a client. The
photography portfolios that follow highlight
a wide range of talent.

'I am a professional photographer, and a science and math teacher at a middle school in Southern California. It is a great combination, allowing me to have summers off to do art shows and work full time on my photography. Before I became a teacher, I worked as a land surveyor and photogrammetrist, focusing on photography as a tool for making measurements, rather than photography as fine art. I have been a photographer for many years, but only after discovering the Polaroid transfer technique was it that I turned my hobby into a business.

I've been in business about three years, and on-line about five months.'

Artist's Statement:

The focus of my work is Polaroid transfer photography, including image and emulsion transfers. I create limited edition fine art photographs of flowers, landscapes, seascapes, cityscapes and still life. Before I launched my website, I was selling my photography mainly at art shows in the Southern California area in the USA.

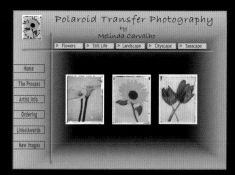 

 How many hits on the site do you get per week?
I am getting approximately 250 hits per week currently, but the numbers are increasing as my website continues to be listed higher on the major search engines such as Google, Yahoo, Lycos, and AOL.

 On a scale of 1 to 10, how would you rate its effectiveness in obtaining clients?
Two for individuals who have never seen my artwork in person, and an eight for people who have seen and/or purchased my art at shows. My website has been more successful in obtaining contacts from art professionals and publishing companies and less successful in generating direct sales to the public.

 How do you distribute information about where to access your portfolio?
I distribute business cards at my shows that have my Web link on them. When I sell greeting cards, I have a Web link on the back of the card. I send postcards to my clients announcing upcoming events; these also include a Web link to my site. I am listed on many search engines on the Internet. I also have approximately 30 reciprocal links on various photography websites/on-line galleries that link back to my Web page.

 Did you work with a Web designer to create the website? If so, who was the designer?
My boyfriend (Steve Knapp) and I designed and created the website using Adobe Photoshop, Ulead Smartsaver Pro, Macromedia's Fireworks and Dreamweaver.

 Do you have a CD or disk version of the portfolio that you distribute?
Yes, upon request.

Rui received a degree in graphic design in 1995 in Weisbaden, Germany, and has been working as a freelance photographer since then. Rui has been on-line since August 2000.

Artist's Statement:
My main focus is people, portrait and reportage, but I enjoy setting it aside occasionally to explore fashion and still life photography.

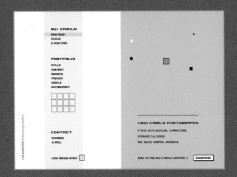
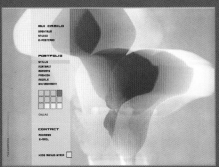

 How many hits on the site do you get per week?
On average 2,500 different IPs (I get many more hits, but about 2,500 different people visit weekly).

 On a scale of 1 to 10, how would you rate its effectiveness in obtaining clients?
Nine, compared to all the other possibilities a photographer has.

 How do you distribute information about where to access your portfolio?
Because of the numerous awards the site has won – I hope it doesn't sound like I'm showing off. I didn't win the awards; it was the design agency Scholz & Volkmer in Weisbaden, Germany. They created my site – the information about where to access my portfolio has spread like an avalanche. I got an incredible amount of feedback in the first half year, and it is still a lot. So, it's definitely worth it to take care of a good design, and maybe send it into some design competitions. Word of mouth can be very powerful.

 Did you work with a Web designer to create the website? If so, who was the designer?
The site was created by the agency Scholz & Volkmer in Wiesbaden, Germany (www.s-v.de).

 Do you have a CD or disk version of the portfolio that you distribute?
No, because I like to change pictures quite often. I prefer to use my newsletter to inform customers about new pictures. It's also a good way to keep in contact.

Jonathan Greet / Dominic Ibbotson
dumdum.co.uk – www.dumdum.co.uk

dumdum.co.uk was established in 2000. They have been on-line since the beginning of 2000.

Artist's Statement:

dumdum.co.uk is an Edinburgh-based design company specialising in providing complete corporate packages of print, Web and photography. Dominic Ibbotson and Jonathan Greet, who are both graduates of Photography, Film and Television, formed the company. As well as tackling a multitude of commercial projects dumdum are involved in various arts projects and support roles for other artists and photographers.

How many hits on the site do you get per week?
On average we get about 400 hits a week, this is dropping off a little so we'll have to do a bit more search engine promotion and optimisation.

On a scale of 1 to 10, how would you rate its effectiveness in obtaining clients?
On the photography side of the business it works very well (eight out of ten) creating about $1000 per month from clients based in the UK and the States. People are often looking for photographers close to their required location to avoid travelling expenses. I think our location in Edinburgh that has lots of international events and conferences helps.

The Web side of the business doesn't do as good from the website (four out of ten). One reason for this is that Web developers are much more knowledgeable about search engine promotion compared to photographers, so there is much more competition.

How do you distribute information about where to access your portfolio?
As a small company word of mouth is still probably our most important marketing tool.

Did you work with a Web designer to create the website? If so, who was the designer?
We designed the site ourselves using Flash, Dreamweaver, Illustrator and Photoshop.

Do you have a CD or disk version of the portfolio that you distribute?
We do have a version on disk although we normally point people towards our site. We also use PDFs quite a lot and have various targeted portfolios depending on the type of work the client is looking for.

Tim has been in business for 30 years and has been on-line for a year and a half.

Artist's Statement:

I am a freelance photographer. I am based in Arizona and have photographed on assignment in three continents and in most major (and a number of minor) American cities for corporate, advertising, magazine and book publishing clients.

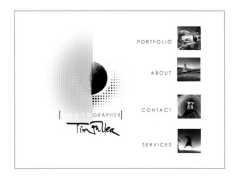

 How many hits on the site do you get per week?
I don't know.

 On a scale of 1 to 10, how would you rate its effectiveness in obtaining clients?
I'm not sure but I know that some people that have hired me have mentioned they did so because of my website.

 How do you distribute information about where to access your portfolio?
Word of mouth and on my business cards.

 Did you work with a Web designer to create the website? If so, who was the designer?
My assistant designed it in conjunction with a Web designer as a consultant. We used GoLive.

 Do you have a CD or disk version of the portfolio that you distribute?
No.

Rob has been a photographer for ten years. The site has been on-line for six months.

Artist's Statement:

I am an educator, photographer and artist: I split my work into several distinct arenas. As an educator the main emphasis is on the transference of skills, understanding and communication.

As a commercial image-maker, the emphasis is to use the skills and understanding (built over time) to achieve work that satisfies the client and in the process produces something that excites and meets their requirements.

Finally the fine art work that I pursue tends to be issue-based and can be a form of catharsis. The subject matter for this work is drawn from personal experience.

All aspects of my work overlap and occasionally the difference is hard to define. In many ways this allows for a much wider range of clients.

 How many hits on the site do you get per week?
140 hits per week.

 On a scale of 1 to 10, how would you rate its effectiveness in obtaining clients?
As this site has been launched only recently, the amount of interest that it has generated has been minimal, with enquiries happening on a weekly basis rather than a daily basis. This should pick up when other forms of direct marketing are applied.

 How do you distribute information about where to access your portfolio?
The main distribution of information about the website happens in several ways, which include word of mouth, direct contact with agents and commissioning editors, and a blanket distribution of CD versions of the website to potentially interested parties.

 Did you work with a Web designer to create the website? If so, who was the designer?
The website was constructed by David Viney, with input design from myself. It was a joint effort. I find that if you work with other people then the results tend to be more rounded and cohesive, especially if there is extreme honesty involved.

 Do you have a CD or disk version of the portfolio that you distribute?
Yes there is a CD version of the website, which is updated regularly.

Geoff has been in business for three years as a freelance professional and has been on-line for two years.

Artist's Statement:
I am a stock and assignment photographer based in Flagstaff, Arizona in the USA. I shoot action, adventure and travel photography for advertising and editorial usage. I also do fine art landscapes and portraits. My medium is 35mm.

 How many hits on the site do you get per week?
1120 hits per week; 63 visitors per week.

 On a scale of 1 to 10, how would you rate its effectiveness in obtaining clients?
Five.

 How do you distribute information about where to access your portfolio?
Email, telephone, promotional mailings and enquiries from Web users.

 Did you work with a Web designer to create the website? If so, who was the designer?
No. I designed it with Adobe GoLive 4.0.

 Do you have a CD or disk version of the portfolio that you distribute?
Yes.

Max has been in business for 12 years. His portfolio has been on-line for six months.

Artist's Statement:
Most of all I'm a photographer for architecture and interiors. But I do also some studio work – for example technical stills for the computer industry – and twice a year the CPD (the world's biggest fashion fair).

 How many hits on the site do you get per week?
40.

 On a scale of 1 to 10, how would you rate its effectiveness in obtaining clients?
Five.

 How do you distribute information about where to access your portfolio?
Word of mouth, Redbox and links from other sites.

 Did you work with a Web designer to create the website? If so, who was the designer?
My son, Janek Ruessmann created the site. He used Flash and Dreamweaver.
J.ruessmann@web.de.

 Do you have a CD or disk version of the portfolio that you distribute?
No.

Jensen has been in business for five years and has been on-line for two years.

Artist's Statement:
I am an advertising and editorial photographer. I focus on people. That's my passion. I get a rush from it. Being one on one with a person and getting that expression that you're not necessarily looking for. Stopping that 1/250 of a second. You've captured it. That's great. I like to get to know someone, watch body language. I have about ten minutes to get to know my subject. That's challenging and I like a challenge.

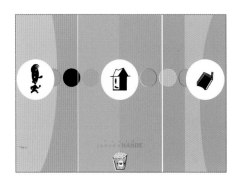

 How many hits on the site do you get per week?
I don't know.

 On a scale of 1 to 10, how would you rate its effectiveness in obtaining clients?
By itself three, with other resources maybe a seven. I still have to send in my book.

 How do you distribute information about where to access your portfolio?
I use direct mail, business cards, source books, credit lines (instead of your name sometimes I use my URL), and www.portfolios.com with a link. I find that pretty effective. I have got several jobs with the use of other portfolio websites. I don't have the time or money to register with every search engine nowadays. If I need to put up new work it is easily done with the portfolio sites. The learning curve doesn't kill me. I can put up Polaroids of a shoot that I'm working on to get feedback from the client. Photoserve is interesting me right now. I will probably register with them and put up a portfolio with my link. Maybe put a little different work on that site. I'm not a Web designer or a computer programmer. I would much rather be behind my camera than my computer. It's getting harder and harder to do that these days.

 Did you work with a Web designer to create the website? If so, who was the designer?
I worked with a fantastic designer called Robert Haines. I had a general idea about how I wanted it to look and be navigated. He was great at telling me what I couldn't do. He kept me grounded and tweaked stuff that added a lot to the site.

 Do you also have a CD or disk version of the portfolio that you distribute?
No. I think that's too much to ask the art director to do. Too much time is involved for them to look at it.

Julian has been in business for 20 years and on-line for five years.

Artist's Statement:
I specialise in doing portraiture and still life photography for corporate, publishing, editorial, design and advertising clients both in the studio and on location. More detail can be found on my website.

How many hits on the site do you get per week?
I don't know.

On a scale of 1 to 10, how would you rate its effectiveness in obtaining clients?
I'd rate it four: its main use is as a further reference for existing and potential clients to see examples of my work, to showcase personal projects and to upload specific items for a select group of clients to see. It works in conjunction with visits to clients with a hard copy portfolio.

How do you distribute information about where to access your portfolio?
Email, visits, word of mouth, PDFs, etc.

Did you work with a Web designer to create the website? If so, who was the designer?
The designer is Ian Campodonic, icampodonic@btinternet.com.

Do you also have a CD or disk version of the portfolio that you distribute?
This is currently in production and I hope to have it available by the end of 2002.

Steve's been in business, including education since 1991. He's worked as a freelancer with his own studio since 1994 and has been on-line since March 2001.

Artist's Statement:
I am a commercial photographer with my main focus in people, beauty, fashion, editorial, lifestyle etc. I own a stock agency (www.deepol.com) and I'm a studio partner of Rui Camilo.

 How many hits on the site do you get per week?
Total hits since being on-line: 110,000. Hits per week are around 900–1,000.

 On a scale of 1 to 10, how would you rate its effectiveness in obtaining clients?
Three or four.

 How do you distribute information about where to access your portfolio?
I use search engines, email (mailing), directories, postcards (direct mail), links, awards, publications and so on.

 Did you work with a Web designer to create the website? If so, who was the designer?
The designers were Michael Nixdorf (m.nixdorf@deepol.com) and Roman Holt (roman.holt@heliumdesign.de), and the programmers were Michael Nixdorf and Mathias Schaab (www.webraum.de).

 Do you have a CD or disk version of the portfolio that you distribute?
No, not yet, but I'm thinking about it.

Bryan has been in business for four years and has had his portfolio on-line for a year.

Artist's Statement:

People are the main focus within my photography. I'm mainly concerned with getting an interesting or humorous portrait, either through gestures or by telling a small story. I tend to work primarily in colour for my advertising, music, and fashion work. Usually shooting with a very loud and energetic style always looking for the unexpected. People don't want to see regurgitated imagery, so I'm always looking for the alternative. Photography has been very good to me.

There is nothing better than hanging out with cool people, laughing, being obnoxious, breaking things and shooting amazing imagery. The sweetest part is when someone hires you for a similar job, as they respect what you can capture and invoke within the subjects. When the art directors trust you with full creative control and freedom, the ceiling has been raised and they're just waiting for you to smash through it, exceeding expectations and creating award-winning imagery. Therefore everyone wins, my basic dream job.

 How many hits on the site do you get per week?
70 to 100.

 On a scale of 1 to 10, how would you rate its effectiveness in obtaining clients?
Eight.

 How do you distribute information about where to access your portfolio?
Through direct mail, email, promotional pieces, word of mouth, business cards, and with my portfolio.

 Did you work with a Web designer to create the website? If so, who was the designer?
Yes, the designer was Arun Chateurvedi, and the programmer was Eric Purino.

 Do you have a CD or disk version of the portfolio that you distribute?
I distribute an email package consisting of JPEG images that the client would be interested in i.e. a fashion package or an advertising package, etc.

Jimmy has been taking photographs of jazz musicians for 11 years. His portfolio has been on-line for three and a half years.

Artist's Statement:
The purpose of my work is to document, in an artistic fashion, the only genuine American art form, jazz. I have done this for the past 11 years in the jazz capital of the world, New York City. I have been involved in over 250 CD projects, and have done more than 20 magazine covers. My photographs have appeared in The New York Times, People Magazine, Time Magazine, Jazz Times Swing Journal and Ken Burn's Jazz. I have had a number of one-man shows and have lectured on portrait photography and jazz.

How many hits on the site do you get per week?
400.

On a scale of 1 to 10, how would you rate its effectiveness in obtaining clients?
Seven.

How do you distribute information about where to access your portfolio?
Direct mail and word of mouth.

Did you work with a Web designer to create the website? If so, who was the designer?
I worked with three Web designers, Sputnik, Ned Otter and David Leonard. For a small website, my site is unique. My site was built with zero HTML maintenance in mind. This was achieved via modification of an access database from a Web form.

Do you have a CD or disk version of the portfolio that you distribute?
No, my images are stolen often enough. I don't need to facilitate the process by handing out CDs of my work! I like the speed and convenience of electronically transmitting images and I can control the resolution of my images by regulating my file sizes.

Estelle has been in business since January 2000 and went on-line at the same time.

Artist's Statement:
I am not specialised in a certain genre of photography. I like everything that can be photographed. I am addicted to photography and always carry a camera with me.

 How many hits on the site do you get per week?
Up to 1,500.

 On a scale of 1 to 10, how would you rate its effectiveness in obtaining clients?
Seven.

 How do you distribute information about where to access your portfolio?
For client mailing I have many listings in on-line design forums and magazines, this spreads in a Ping-Pong effect.

 Did you work with a Web designer to create the website? If so, who was the designer?
Art direction and design was by Torsten Mauss, Duesseldorf, Germany (mauss@eentwee.de/www.eentwee.de).

 Do you also have a CD or disk version of the portfolio that you distribute?
No.

'I have been a freelancer since 1999, beginning with smaller jobs for record companies and editorials when still a student. Since obtaining my diploma, I have worked as a full-time freelancer in the German market as well as abroad. I consider myself a very motivated newcomer. My portfolio has been on-line since January 2001 and will be relaunched in October 2002.'

Artist's Statement:
The focus of my work is people photography, fashion, interiors, advertisements and film stills. I like to take part in picture composing and in the organisation of photo productions. I also enjoy working with different people because I very much value the artistic stimulation and exchange of ideas that networking can provide. In my opinion, networking means many small cells of creativity and information becoming one in the sense that the whole is always more than the sum of its single parts – which of course depends on the focus of the job. To be a photo-designer it is not only taking pictures.

 How many hits on the site do you get per week?
That depends on what I do. If I have a publication in an editorial/magazine/film the people who read or see this and are interested want to see more and click on my site. Sometimes that is 200 times a week, sometimes only 50.

 On a scale of 1 to 10, how would you rate its effectiveness in obtaining clients?
I would say maybe five or six because an on-line portfolio is like an archive. People who are interested in what I do get the chance to evaluate my work, my style or the aesthetics of my pictures at their own pace. Yet I think that it's still necessary to meet your clients face-to-face. Clients usually want to know what kind of person you are and how you work. On-line portfolios are more like a fast overview of one's style.

 How do you distribute information about where to access your portfolio?
Of course I use direct mail when contacting my existing and potential clients, usually in the form of small newsletters. For our association we have a special newsletter system. I also talk to a lot of people and give them information by word of mouth. And I collect meticulously all information in a mailing list. I spend plenty of time with distribution, collecting information and preparing newsletters and hand-outs for agencies.

 Did you work with a Web designer to create the website? If so, who was the designer?
The conception and the design of my website was done by me. Preparing an on-line portfolio was part of my studies and I found it very challenging to come up with a concept and design that would best present the assets of my work. A friend of mine then programmed the site according to my wishes.

 Do you also have a CD or disk version of the portfolio that you distribute?
Yes I do. Each client or agency I work with gets one CD with all the valid information. I even give out CDs to people who are potentially interested in my work.

Edward has been in business for 25 years and on-line for six years.

Artist's Statement:
I am a location photographer specialising in annual report, corporate, editorial and public relations photography. Shooting takes me across the USA, with some international travel.

 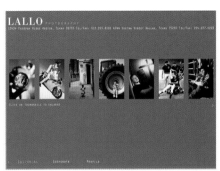

 How many hits on the site do you get per week?
30 to 40.

 On a scale of 1 to 10, how would you rate its effectiveness in obtaining clients?
It is only a one in obtaining clients, however, the main purpose of my site is to let potential clients that I have contacted have a quick place to view my portfolio without having to courier a hard copy.

 How do you distribute information about where to access your portfolio?
Mostly word of mouth, it is also on my business cards and all promotional pieces.

 Did you work with a Web designer to create the website? If so, who was the designer?
Yes, the designer was a now defunct Austin, Texas agency in the USA.

 Do you also have a CD or disk version of the portfolio that you distribute?
Yes.

Steve has been in business for 22 years and has been on-line for two years.

Artist's Statement:
I am a general commercial photographer specialising in people on location. I do, however, have pages for my architectural, stills and stock photography on my site.

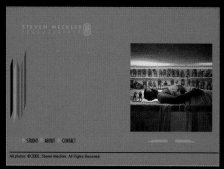

How many hits on the site do you get per week?
We don't track this.

On a scale of 1 to 10, how would you rate its effectiveness in obtaining clients?
We don't expect or get many unsolicited new clients directly from the site. Our main function for the site is to provide immediate information to referred clients. We also use it to provide information to studio rental clients.

How do you distribute information about where to access your portfolio?
Direct mail and word of mouth. We've also used source books, the ASMP website with a link to ours and an on-line portfolio site that is also linked to ours.
.

Did you work with a Web designer to create the website? If so, who was the designer?
You don't want to know. It was a miserable experience. Suffice it to say that this designer was under experienced.

If you designed it yourself, what software did you use?
After my initial fiasco, I designed it myself and then worked with a very good Web builder who put it together.

Chris has been in business for 22 years and on-line for four years.

Artist's Statement:
I'm a professional photographer shooting people and products in Tucson, Arizona, USA. The work I'm most known for is the sports posters I've produced for local sporting events and the University of Arizona. My work is heavily influenced and manipulated by digital imaging. I started working with digital in 1994 and never looked back.

 How many hits on the site do you get per week?
I don't know.

 On a scale of 1 to 10, how would you rate its effectiveness in obtaining clients?
Two.

 How do you distribute information about where to access your portfolio?
Word of mouth. I use my website to show my portfolio to potential clients who have called the studio looking for samples of my work.

 Did you work with a Web designer to create the website? If so, who was the designer?
Yes, Samual Macomber.

 Do you have a CD or disk version of the portfolio that you distribute?
No.

Kimm has been in business for three and a half years. The portfolio has been on-line since the beginning of 2000 and together with two friends Kimm has also started a design agency called Sigarett (www.sigarett.com).

Artist's Statement:
I am a freelance photographer based in Norway, concentrating on editorial work for magazines and commercial work for advertising agencies. I just try to have fun no matter what the assignment.

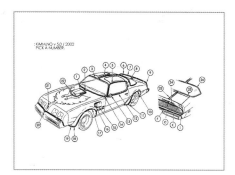

 How many hits on the site do you get per week?
I average 169, though the highest was 2,400.

 On a scale of 1 to 10, how would you rate its effectiveness in obtaining clients?
Maybe a six. My site is quite personal (as a freelance photographer), it includes all kinds of photography, the stuff that I love to do, and so it is not made solely for getting commercial jobs.

 How do you distribute information about where to access your portfolio?
Through direct mail, email, and then word of mouth I guess. A lot of other people and sites have linked me up on their pages.

 Did you work with a Web designer to create the website? If so, who was the designer?
I did it myself as I have a minor in graphic design from AAC, SF. I used Adobe Photoshop, Adobe ImageReady, Adobe Streamline, and Macromedia Dreamweaver.

 Do you also have a CD or disk version of the portfolio that you distribute?
No, not at the moment.

Ron has been in business for seven years.
He's been on-line for three years.

Artist's Statement:
I do commercial photography ranging from people to still life.

 How many hits on the site do you get per week?
30 to 50.

 On a scale of 1 to 10, how would you rate its effectiveness in obtaining clients?
Six.

 How do you distribute information about where to access your portfolio?
Direct mail, direct emails, phone calls, business cards and Web portfolios on a portfolio centre (www.portfolios.com) where I believe most of my hits come from; people click through this site to my site.

 Did you work with a Web designer to create the website? If so, who was the designer?
I designed it myself with Freehand mainly, and with Photoshop and Illustrator as support.

Tom has been in business for 22 years.

Artist's Statement:
Currently I work from film originals exclusively, which are often preferred over digital files by the publishers who license my photographs. I use high-resolution scans to bring these images into the 'digital darkroom' for enhanced creative control in print-making. An interdisciplinary background in art and science has fuelled my passion for insightful images focused on the mystery, beauty, and complexity of the natural world. I usually work in colour and have an endless fascination with the ephemeral – as brief as a lightning flash or as 'long' as a desert wildflower bloom – and am now producing huge panoramic prints for home and corporate decor. Although my files include some haunting images that reflect our loss of harmony with the world about us, I prefer to focus on subjects that will rekindle a sense of wonder in us all.

How many hits on the site do you get per week?
My Web portfolio has been on-line for about one year and receives an average of 3,050 hits per week by approximately 269 visitors per week, with each visit averaging seven minutes in duration.

On a scale of 1 to 10, how would you rate its effectiveness in obtaining clients?
I've not yet attempted to measure the effectiveness of the site in attracting new clients, something that's very difficult to quantify. At this stage, the site functions more as a public relations tool than as a sales venue. When someone expresses interest in my work, it's super-convenient to steer them to a URL that provides an overview of who I am and what I do.

How do you distribute information about where to access your portfolio?
My Web address appears on my business cards, at the bottom of all email correspondence, in professional trade directories (printed and on-line), and in press coverage whenever possible.

Did you work with a Web designer to create the website? If so, who was the designer?
The site was designed by Michael Robinson and Katerina Munzar, using Dreamweaver and Photoshop software.

Do you have a CD or disk version of the portfolio that you distribute?
I regularly prepare customised CDs expanded from my Web portfolio, each tailored to the interests of the client. A CD with sample images from my latest independently published book – The Southwest Inside Out – accompanies our press releases, which increases the likelihood of getting media coverage.

Art Directors

This group of graphics professionals is the mind behind the designs. They envision the concept, and find the right talent to make their vision a reality. They are in the position to say yay or nay to your portfolio. Many started their careers as graphic designers, illustrators or photographers and know the ropes behind the creative process. They often are driven creative types who thrive on long hours and espresso. Here you'll find some of the websites of their agencies.

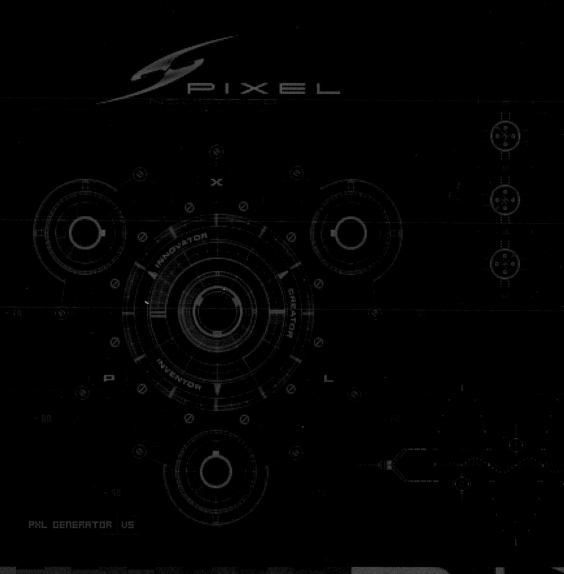

Anthony Amidei, Steve Barretto, Stephen Jaycox

Perimetre-Flux – www.perimetre-flux.com

Perimetre-Flux has been in business since 1998. This version of their site has been on-line since 2001.

Artists' Statement:
Our design studio is young, versatile and accomplished. We are a studio of 16 people, capable of conducting business fluently in multiple languages, and more importantly, benefit from the richness of this diversity as it critically informs each project we produce. As one might expect from a studio with such diversity, no single graphic language prevails and this fact supports our belief that the work that we produce for each client is necessarily unique. We believe that our role as designers is to draw out the client's voice, and not to substitute it with our own.

How many hits on the site do you get per week?
Approximately 250.

On a scale of 1 to 10, how would you rate its effectiveness in obtaining clients?
Five. As one might expect, because we are a small studio most of our effort goes into client projects, so our own site is always the last priority it seems.

How do you distribute information about where to access your portfolio?
Because we work in high press profile markets (museums, etc.) our site promotion is usually in tandem with the promotional efforts of our clients. We do notice a boost in traffic after, say, a major exhibition opens that we have done some work for.

Did you work with a Web designer to create the website? If so, who was the designer?
We are primarily a design and strategy studio, so all of the design was done in-house. Our designer uses Adobe Illustrator and Adobe Photoshop. The site itself was hand-coded by our technology designers.

Do you also have a CD or disk version of the portfolio that you distribute?
We have assembled projects on CD-ROM or DVD from time to time for client review, but there is no 'product' that we send out per se.

What are the key factors in choosing an artist, or photographer for a particular job?
We look for design partners that are able to quickly understand, and work productively within the visual languages native to our client accounts. It is important to us that the work we produce on our client's behalf bears their fingerprint, and not necessarily our own. The design and creative fields are largely populated by talent that has developed their 'own style' and hope to sell that style to clients. We find multi-faceted designers much more capable as partners in the kinds of projects we produce.

What do you like to see in a digital portfolio?
A trace of a thought process, a critical re-evaluation of previous work; neither of which is directly illustrated by our own site, but that is what we ourselves, aspire to.

Vince Frost

Frost design – www.frostdesign.co.uk

Vincent has been in business since 1994 when he formed his own consultancy and on-line for two years.

Artist's Statement:
My work is known for its innovative use of photographic images and striking typography.

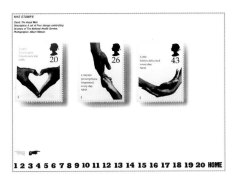

 How many hits on the site do you get per week?
200.

 On a scale of 1 to 10, how would you rate its effectiveness in obtaining clients?
It brings in a few, however, we mainly use it as an on-line portfolio.

 How do you distribute information about where to access your portfolio?
Frost mailer, word of mouth, press cuttings, lectures and judging.

 Did you work with a Web designer to create the website? If so, who was the designer?
I designed it with Dreamweaver.

 Do you have a CD or disk version of the portfolio that you distribute?
Yes, the Frost Slide Show.

 What are the key factors in choosing an artist, or photographer for a particular job?
Relevance.

 What do you like to see in a digital portfolio?
Good work.

Matilda has been in business for six years and on-line for eight months.

Artist's Statement:

My work encompasses both traditional and digital methods of creation. Formally, it includes both fine art and illustration, and conceptually, it aims to reach both artistic and the scientific audiences. The thread that holds all of this together is that the work is representational – realist. Interdisciplinary/diverse/eclectic – welcome to the 21st century. My work is an expression of the times in which I live: having grown up with only traditional media, trained in the most antiquated styles of painting and drawing possible, I crossed the digital divide with oil paint and charcoal in my toolbox. Now I am able to bring sensibilities back and forth from one to the other. I firmly believe that experiential knowledge of traditional materials is critical to well rounded visual creation – be it digital or otherwise.

 How many hits on the site do you get per week?
15–30.

 On a scale of 1 to 10, how would you rate its effectiveness in obtaining clients?
I don't think the site gets my clients alone, but it is an excellent tool that sells my experience and abilities after I, or someone on my behalf, have made preliminary contact. It continues to function as a reference tool for discussion about style, format etc., while working on projects.

 How do you distribute information about where to access your portfolio?
Word of mouth and the URL is on my business cards.

 Did you work with a Web designer to create the website? If so, who was the designer?
I designed it myself using FrontPage.

 Do you also have a CD or disk version of the portfolio that you distribute?
No other digital means, but I still have a paper/hard copy portfolio too.

 What are the key factors in choosing an artist, or photographer for a particular job?
Versatility, past performance, appropriateness of style to subject, punctuality.

 What do you like to see in a digital portfolio?
Versatility and depth of development in a particular direction. Soulfulness in the work.

Jas Denny

HSAG Design – www.hsag.co.uk

HSAG was originally formed in 1964. It has been on-line for five years.

Artist's Statement:

HSAG is one of the UK's most experienced design consultancies. Since 1964 we have helped literally hundreds of organisations in business, industry and the public sector to communicate more effectively. Through the intelligent use of design, words and images, HSAG Design creates identities and award-winning communications that impress and persuade its target audiences.

Our approach focuses on two main principles. First, we operate in the 'real world': fully understanding the business context and aims of our client's communication. Secondly, the creative solutions we develop reflect, above all else, 'intelligence'. Good design, we believe, is basically the intelligent organisation of ideas. For creative inspiration we draw on both high technology and traditional craftsmanship, avant garde styles and classical typography, free-form graphics and rigorous systems.

Our work demonstrates creativity that is driven by client need, rather than by fashion or fleeting trends. The value we add is to create communications in a new and different light – one that makes the audience more interested in, and receptive to the client's message.

The application of extensive skills and knowledge, with direct responsibility of project management by creative professionals ensures originality and quality.

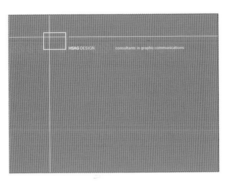

How many hits on the site do you get per week?
2,000.

On a scale of 1 to 10, how would you rate its effectiveness in obtaining clients?
Two.

How do you distribute information about where to access your portfolio?
The URL is on our stationery and brochures. In all new business contacts we make we tell people we have a website. Key word 'design' on search engines probably generates most hits.

Did you work with a Web designer to create the website? If so, who was the designer?
No, we built it ourselves using BBEdit (HTML), Photoshop, and Illustrator.

Do you have a CD or disk version of the portfolio that you distribute?
No.

What are the key factors in choosing an artist, or photographer for a particular job?
Style of work, suitability to the subject, existing examples of similar work.

Marc founded his company Pixel:Industries – the art of visual communication – in 1995. Before that time he mainly worked as a freelance designer in print media. He started designing when he was 13 years old. The portfolio of his personal website has been on-line since the end of 1999.

Artist's Statement:
I think the main focus of my work is to concentrate on the more or less 'experimental' part of my daily design work; the possibility to experiment with new shapes and forms in combination with typography and literature.

 How many hits on the site do you get per week?
Weekly hits for my personal home page vary between 50,000–65,000.

 On a scale of 1 to 10, how would you rate its effectiveness in obtaining clients?
I suggest three. The main reason why I decided to put some of my artwork on my personal website was to share inspiration rather than the possibility to obtain new clients. I see my personal website more or less as a so-called 'fun project'.

 How do you distribute information about where to access your portfolio?
Word of mouth first of all.

 Did you work with a Web designer to create the website? If so, who was the designer?
No. I programmed the website all by myself. I used Adobe GoLive for the creation of my own website project, as well as my client projects. I have been doing beta-testing for several of Adobe's software applications such as, Adobe GoLive, Adobe ImageReady, and Adobe Photoshop.

 Do you have a CD or disk version of the portfolio that you distribute?
No, I have no other digital media archive except my website to expose my digital design artworks. I mainly use hard copies of my portfolio if I have client meetings. A piece of paper is still a very impressive manner of presenting your portfolio.

 What are the key factors in choosing an artist, or photographer for a particular job?
I usually do not engage any design artist, illustrator or photographer for a specific job due to the fact that I mainly do everything by myself. This guarantees the most creative freedom and quality of my finished design works.

 What do you like to see in a digital portfolio?
All artworks where the spectator is able to feel the 'joy of creating' the artworks presented. Any kind of artwork which reflects a certain 'emotion' or 'frame of mind'.

Liam has been in business for one and a half years at hey moscow and five years in website design. The hey moscow website has been on-line since the inception.

Artist's Statement:

hey moscow's strength is giving personality to brands and the way they communicate – making them stand out from the increasing noise out there. With websites, we try to create highly functional sites that generate return on investment for the client.

 How many hits on the site do you get per week?
300–400.

 On a scale of 1 to 10, how would you rate its effectiveness in obtaining clients?
Two.

 How do you distribute information about where to access your portfolio?
Follow up to sales calls, ads/listings in relevant directories, collateral we produce, DM, e-shots and press coverage.

 Did you work with a Web designer to create the website? If so, who was the designer?
Andy Green – co-director using Dreamweaver, Flash, Photoshop, and Infini-D.

 Do you also have a CD or disk version of the portfolio that you distribute?
No, we have our brochure which contains photographs in juxtaposed contexts of our work.

 What are the key factors in choosing an artist, or photographer for a particular job?
Creativity and enthusiasm, plus an ability to think for themselves. We DON'T want 'yes men'.

 What do you like to see in a digital portfolio?
Variety, creativity, innovation and effectiveness.

Antti Hinkula and Teemu Suviala have been in business for about eight years. They founded their company, Syrup Helsinki in October 2001. Before Syrup they studied and worked as freelance designers. The Syrup Helsinki portfolio has been on-line for nine months.

Artist's Statement:
We are a visual communications studio; our mission is to produce innovative visual concepts for a variety of clients and make the world a beautiful place.

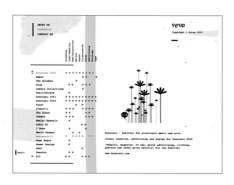
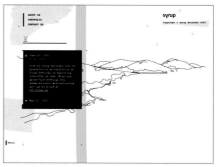

How many hits on the site do you get per week?
5,000–10,000.

On a scale of 1 to 10, how would you rate its effectiveness in obtaining clients?
Eight.

How do you distribute information about where to access your portfolio?
Our site has been presented many times in different design portals on the Web since we went on-line. I think that has been one of the best ways of distributing information abroad. Several publications have written about our work and us too.

Did you work with a Web designer to create the website? If so, who was the designer?
We created the site. We design in every format, we do a lot of print but also a lot of Web and motion graphics. For us the format makes no difference, we do everything by ourselves, also programming.

Do you have a CD or disk version of the portfolio that you distribute?
We have a printed portfolio and also a CD version.

What are the key factors in choosing an artist, or photographer for a particular job?
Style and expression. Before we hire anyone for any job, we have a certain style, and way of expression in our minds. After we get the image in our heads, we look up the person who can do that. We use lots of photographers for different projects. Most of the other creative work (concept design, art, graphic design, illustrating etc.) we do by ourselves.

What do you like to see in a digital portfolio?
In a digital portfolio it's usually easy to show all the work which is originally designed for digital formats (websites, motion graphics, animations, etc.). It's not so often that you see printed stuff presented very well in a digital portfolio. That's what we would like to see – and what we are going to try for on our next site – a digital portfolio where printed graphics have been presented in a perfect way.

Tel Design was founded in 1962. The actual portfolio went on-line in the middle of 2002, however, its corporate presentation includes portfolio-like matter such as exemplary logos and examples of recent projects. The site in this version has existed for three years; its first version went on-line in 1995.

Artist's Statement:
Tel Design is a well-known Dutch agency, specialising in the design and development of visual identities. We tackle our field of work in a conceptual manner, provide our clients with strategic and communicational argumentations to connect position to identity and branding, and develop the identity in the areas of information design, editorial design, environmental design and new media design.

How many hits on the site do you get per week?
Total hits vary around a hundred a week; relevant hits (people actually looking for information on design or design agencies or us specifically) are estimated to be between 20 and 30.

On a scale of 1 to 10, how would you rate its effectiveness in obtaining clients?
Difficult to answer; The only measure we have on the effectiveness of the site is asking people we actually get in contact with if they have seen our site, which in most cases they have.

How do you distribute information about where to access your portfolio?
Apart from the usual distribution of the URL on our stationery and business cards, and mentioning the site as much as possible, we send a so-called 'Tel-email' and 'Tel-e-fax' on a regular basis, and include references to the site in the 'Tel-flyer' that we send out now and then.

Did you work with a Web designer to create the website? If so, who was the designer?
We used a freelance Web designer from Germany, Niels Buenemann, for the actual production, but apart from that we did it all ourselves: concept, design, text and content. Animated illustrations were worked out by Niels on the basis of original artwork by Petra Esveld. Concept, text and design were done by Peter Post and undersigned.

Do you also have a CD or disk version of the portfolio that you distribute?
No.

What are the key factors in choosing an artist, or photographer for a particular job?
That he or she fits. He or she must understand the problem, be capable of solving it and be happy under our supervision.

What do you like to see in a digital portfolio?
Clarity. I want to get a clear picture of what the work is about, how it was conceived, by what method of working etc. You should be able to judge by a portfolio if this is the artist for your job, and if this artist will be good to work with.

Figure 4.1
www.portfolios.com.

Figure 4.2
www.Photoserve.com.

Figure 4.3
www.designiskinky.net.

Figure 4.4
www.MediaInspiration.com.

Figure 4.5
www.designiskinky.net.

Figure 4.6
www.CoolHomePages.com.

Figure 4.7
www.threeoh.com.

Figure 4.8
www.commarts.com.

You can use links from other sites to provide direct access to your site. You may request that a client give you a credit for an illustration, photograph or design used on their site in the form of a link to your URL. There are also specific websites for the purpose of publishing a version of your portfolio. A popular one is www.portfolios.com (Figure 4.1). For a fee you can create an on-line portfolio and www.portfolios.com will post professional, biographical and contact information. It also has a sophisticated search engine that lets a client find your work based on a name, industry, media, client, brand or keyword. You can keep the site updated and post new images at any time.

A site that has a similar mission but a more esoteric approach to the distribution of information of professional services is www.designiskinky.net (Figure 4.3, 4.5). This site features the work of some of the more outrageous designers, illustrators and photographers in the field.

The Digital Design Journal www.threeoh.com (Figure 4.7) also features the portfolios of selected artists. This e-zine contains a number of interesting content-based articles and the portfolios of selected artists.

www.Photoserve.com (Figure 4.2) is another portal for accessing the portfolios of photographers. The site visitor can access a photographer by name, location or specialty.

www.MediaInspiration.com (Figure 4.4) is a designer's resource, giving you access to links, portfolios and forums. There are also articles, books and useful website templates.

www.CoolHomePages.com (Figure 4.6) is a Web designer's resource that provides links to many commercial arts websites.

www.commarts.com (Figure 4.8) (Communication Arts) is the Web address of the popular graphic arts magazine. The site features resources for designers, illustrators, and art directors.

INDEX

Acknowledgements

Writing a book is by no means a solitary venture. This book would not have been possible without the support and assistance of the many friends who contributed their time and talents to its creation. First, I'd like to thank Natalia Price-Cabrera who planted the seed for its inception and whose encouragement and drive kept me on track. I am grateful to Molly Holzschlag for her encouragement and faith in my skill. Thanks to Sarah Jameson who was essential in corresponding with the graphics professionals who contributed their work to the book. My gratitude is owed to Rich Morgan who researched and outlined much of the information in this book and whose opinions gave me perspective on its scope. Thanks to the many illustrators, designers, photographers and art directors who contributed their art, portfolios and insights to the book. I am extremely grateful to the incredibly talented designers at HSAG, especially Sarah Gleave, Martin Bailey and Jas Denny who from cover to cover did an extraordinary job of designing The Perfect Digital Portfolio. Thanks to the engineers and designers at Adobe Systems, Microsoft, Extensis and Macromedia for their helpful assistance in understanding their products. Thanks to my colleagues at Pima Community College, particularly Dave and Cindy Wing, Dennis Landry, Margo Burwell, Jack Mertes and Patti Gardiner. Thanks to Margo Burwell who assisted in the Flash programming of The Perfect Digital Portfolio website. I also want to thank Liisa Phillips for inspiring me and Tim Fuller for his unwavering friendship and my wife Rebecca and daughter Leah for their patience and support.